SCHOOL BASED MANAGEMENT:

A DETAILED GUIDE FOR SUCCESSFUL IMPLEMENTATION

RICHARD G. NEAL

National Educational Service

Bloomington, Indiana   1991

Copyright 1991 by
National Educational Service
1610 W. Third Street
P.O. Box 8
Bloomington, Indiana 47402

All rights reserved, including the right of reproduction
of this book in whole or in part in any form.

Cover design by Addie Seabarkrob

Printed in the United States of America

ISBN 1-879639-15-7

recycled paper

ABOUT THE AUTHOR

Richard G. Neal is a career educator who has been a teacher from the elementary level to the college graduate level and who has served in many educational management and consultant positions both in the public and the private sector. From 1987-1990 Dr. Neal served as Director of School Based Management for the Prince William County Schools in Virginia. Also active in the area of publications, Dr. Neal is the author of numerous books and many articles in the areas of personnel administration, labor relations, and school management. In addition, he has served as editor of several national newsletters.

Over an extended period of time Dr. Neal has been an active consultant for school boards throughout the United States and Canada, having made presentations in over 250 seminars and conferences. He has been a featured speaker for the National School Boards Association, the American Association of School Administrators, the Association for Supervision and Curriculum Development, the Association of School Business Officials, the National Clearinghouse on School Based Management, the National Academy for School Executives, dozens of state and regional associations of school boards and administrators, as well as a long list of individual school districts and private organizations.

Specializing in the decentralization of school management, Dr. Neal has accumulated vast experience which has given him unique insight into the management model commonly referred to as "school based management." Both theoretician and practitioner in such educational management issues, Dr. Neal has a wide and long reputation for giving audiences workable and high quality information.

ACKNOWLEDGEMENTS

Several people played key roles in bringing this book to completion, and I wish to acknowledge them publicly.

Dr. Edward Kelly, Superintendent of the Prince William County Public Schools, Virginia, instigated school based management in that school district and led the decentralization of that district. Without him I would not have had the opportunity to learn about school based management first-hand, and certainly would not have developed the expertise that made this book possible.

Mrs. Cathy Deane, my assistant, worked with me from the inception of school based management in Prince William County until the project was completed and installed three years later. She prepared from my notes various lecture aids which served as the overall basis for this book. She also prepared a portion of the final text for the publisher. Finally, she took care of endless business details in our other assignments which made it possible for me to focus on substantive matters.

Specific acknowledgement is given to Robert Ferrebee, Associate Superintendent for School Management, Prince William County Public Schools, Virginia, who made a significant contribution to school based management by devising many budgetary documents which have been adapted for use in this book.

I wish to express particular gratitude to the many administrators and supervisors who enrolled in my university graduate classes on school based management. From them I learned much. And I owe much to all administrators and supervisors in the Prince William County School System for the opportunity to have been associated with them—members of a truly great staff.

Finally, my wife, Frankie, was the chief editor of this book, as she has been for the numerous other books and articles I have written. She was able to make needed changes, corrections, and improvements without changing the intent of the text.

Special recognition is owed to Dr. Michael Strembitsky, Superintendent of Schools, Edmonton, Alberta, Canada, who knows more and practices more about good school based management than anyone else in Canada or the United States. Michael got me started and gave me needed advice. For that, I am publicly grateful.

TABLE OF CONTENTS

PAGE

1. Why School Based Management? 1

2. What Makes Good Schools? 7
   Clarity of Purpose 7
   Leadership 8
   Professionalism 9
   Lack of Bureaucratic Control 9
   Owned by Stakeholders 10
   Effective Use of Resources 11
   Competition 11
   Choice 12
   Is School Based Management the Answer? 13

3. School Based Management Defined 17
   Commitment Is Needed 18
   School Based Management Is a Structured
     Decentralized Method of Operating the School
     System 20
   School Based Management Operates within
     Understood Parameters 21
   All Players Must Understand Their Roles 22
   Maximized Resource Effectiveness 23
   The Preponderant Share of the Budget Must Be
     Transferred to the Schools 24
   Appropriate Decision-Making Power Must
     Accompany the Transfer of Funds 24

Funds Must Be Allocated Equitably on a
   Differentiated Per Pupil Allocation 25
Funds Must Be Spent According to the Best
   Interests of Students as Determined by an
   Individual School Plan and Individual School
   Budget 27
School Plans and Budgets Should Result from
   Collaboration among Parents, Faculty,
   Students, and the Principal 28
Thorough Preparation Is Essential 29
The Superintendent Must Approve All School
   Plans and Budgets 31
School Plans Should Be Designed to Carry Out
   Goals of Improved Education 31
Evaluation Should Be on Results—Not
   Methodology 32

4. Pros and Cons 35
   There Are Many Advantages to School Based
      Management 35
      Greater commitment by staff to decisions 35
      Greater support for how funds are spent 35
      Increased professional growth 36
      Improvement in morale 36
      The school board and public have a better
         view of spending 37
      More effective spending of limited funds 37
      Educational equity is maximized 38
      "Student based" budgeting is adaptable to
         vouchers and tuition credits 38
      School based management sets a good model
         for students 39
      More leadership opportunity is provided for
         principals 39
      The school becomes more responsive to the
         community 39

    Teachers are empowered for enhanced
        student learning 40

    Educational concerns take highest priority 40

    The educational constituency is enlarged 41

    School based management means "effective
        schools" 42

Does School Based Management Make a
Difference in Student Learning? 43

There Are a Number of Disadvantages to School
Based Management 45

    Preparation requires significant planning
        time and effort 46

    Extra financial assistance is needed to
        finalize a recommendation 46

    Extra time on the part of everybody is
        required initially 46

    The transition will probably involve
        controversy 47

    Labor relations may become a problem 48

    Organizational inefficiency can result 48

    There is no guarantee that things will be
        better 49

School Based Management Can Fail 49

    Failure of the school board to support the
        management system 50

    The superintendent's inability or
        unwillingness to "let go" 51

    The absence of an appropriate organizational
        structure 52

    Unworkable and unfair allocation of
        resources to the schools 52

    Poor labor relations 52

    Inadequate provision of staff development 53

    Customer satisfaction is the acid test of any
        management system 53

    Lack of Preparation 53

5. Requirements for Success 55
    Effective Operation within a Decentralized
        Management Structure 56
    Clear Purpose Understood and Supported by the
        School and Community 57
    Effective Process for Identifying and Adopting
        Goals Aimed at Better Education 58
    Effective Decentralized Management Structure 58
    Clear, Published, and Understood Description of
        Authorities and Responsibilities 58
    Effective Program Planning 59
    Effective Collection and Utilization of Information 59
    Effective Resource Allocation Procedures 59
    Useful Financial Accounting System 60
    Practical Staff Development 60
    Productive Labor Relations 61
    Effective Monitoring Program 61
    Evaluation Program Based on Results—Not
        Methodology 62
    Sound Principles of Organization 63
    High Degree of Satisfaction among Students,
        Parents, and Staff 64

6. Parameters 67
    Responsibility for Activities which have
        Significant, Fluctuating, or Highly
        Unpredictable Costs 72
    Responsibility for Certain Services Needed by the
        School 73

7. Launching the Process 77
    Propose Consideration of School Based
        Management 77

    Establish a Task Force 78
    Determine Guidelines for Task Force 79
    Submit a Recommendation Report 80
    Prepare a Final Report for School Board 80
    The School Board Makes the Final Decision 81
    Sample Motion to Study School Based
        Management 81
    Sample School Board Policy Regarding School
        Based Management 82

8. The School Site Committee 83
    The Committee Must Meet Regularly 84
    The Committee Must Be Involved in the
        Preparation of the School Plan 84
    The Committee Must Be Involved in Preparing
        the School Budget 84
    The Committee Must Serve in an Advisory
        Capacity Regarding Other Important School
        Affairs 84
    The Committee Composition Must Be
        Representative 85
    Committees Can Be Different 85
    The Committees Powers Are Limited 86
    Certain Needs of the Committee Must Be Met 86
    Ground Rules Must Be Established 86
    The Chairperson's Role Must Be Clear 87
    Choosing the Chairperson 87
    An Appropriate Meeting Site Should Be Selected 88
    The Meeting Site Must Be Adequate 88
    Good Communication Is Essential 89
    Westridge Planning Council Bylaws 89

9. School Plan and School Budget 93
    The School Plan and Budget must Fit In with the Planning and Budget Cycles of the School System 93
    The School Plan Should Clearly Describe What Will Be Happening in the School During the Coming School Year 94
    The Format of School Plans Should Be Standardized 95
    The Annual School Plan and Budget Must Be Approved 96
    Approved Budgets Should Not Be Changed 96
    A Sample School Plan Extract 97
        A. The Problem 97
        B. The Proposed Solution 98
        C. Analysis 98
        D. Operational Plan 98
    Sample School Budget under School Based Management 100

10. Student Based Allocation of Funds 103
    Existing System-Wide Average Salaries for Each Employee Classification 104
    Existing and Approved Program Staffing Ratios 105
    Existing and Approved Funding Levels for Programs 105
    Can a School Carry Over Money from Year to Year? . . 107
    What Happens if a School Spends More Than Its Allotted Budget? 107
    Can Principals Transfer Funds within the Approved School Budget? 108
    What Happens if the School System Revenues Are Less Than Called For in the Budget? 109
    Can Schools Purchase Directly from the Private Sector? 109

If Each School Makes Its Own Purchases, Are the
    Economies of Bulk Purchasing Lost? 110
Does the School Based Management Budget
    Process Put More Work on the Principals? 110
Is the Allocation Process 100% Fair? 110
If a School Is Paying Its Own Utilities, Can It
    Keep Its Savings? 111
What Does the Published School System Budget
    Look Like under School Based Management? 111
Must the Amount of Money Allocated to Each
    Student Category Actually Be Spent on Each
    Student in That Category? 112
The Allocation Process 112
Sample Fixed Allocations .114
Sample Staffing Ratios (Elementary School) 116
Sample Staffing Ratios (Middle School) 118
Sample Staffing Ratios (High School) 120
Sample Staffing Ratios (Special Education) 122
Average Salaries 123
Sample Per Pupil Staff Allocation (Grades 1-5) 125
Sample Per Pupil Staff Allocation 126
Sample Student Enrollment 128
Supplies, Equipment & Services 130
Sample Per Pupil Non-Staff Allocation 131
Sample Per Pupil Allocation Factors 133
Sample Elementary School 135
Sample Elementary School Staffing Costs 136
Calculation Sheet 138
Sample Elementary School Based Management
    Budget 140
Sample Middle School Based Management Budget . . .142
Sample High School Based Management Budget 144
Sample Central Office Budget under School Based
    Management 147

    Sample Central Office Budget under School Based
        Management (Elementary Education) 148

    Sample Central Office Budget under School Based
        Management (Library Media Programs) 150

    Sample Central Office Budget (Transportation) 152

    Sample Central Office Budget (Data Processing) 153

    Sample Budget Planning Cycle 154

11. The Pilot Program 155

    Determine the Needed Number of Schools 155

    Determine the Actual Schools for the Program 155

    Allow an Adequate Duration of Time 156

    Establish Limits for the Pilot School 157

    Use a Consultant 158

    Fund the Pilot School the Same as Any Other
        School 158

    Establish the Format and Content of Annual
        School Plans 158

    Establish the Procedure and Format for School
        Budgets 159

    Establish a Financial Accounting Procedure 159

    Include Site Committees in the Pilot Program 159

    Evaluate the Pilot Program 160

    Obtain the Approval of the School Board Prior to
        Implementation 160

12. Evaluation 161

    Preparing to Survey 163

        Why survey? 163

        Who should be surveyed? 164

        Who should write and conduct the survey? 164

        What major activities need to be conducted 164

        What deadlines need to be established? 164

        What is the best time to survey? 164

Choosing the Survey Method 165
Survey Method 165
Preparing the Questionnaire 167
    Never write a question alone 167
    Choose question type carefully 167
    Test the questionnaire for clarity and use 167
    Keep the survey short 167
    The survey should be limited to one topic 167
    Where large numbers of people are being surveyed, the process should be computerized 168
    Do not assume the population understands the topic being surveyed 168
    Delete questions to which the answers can be obtained elsewhere 168
    Avoid hypothetical questions 168
    The student's name should be on the surveys sent to parents 168
    All questionnaires to different groups should share similar questions 168
    Provide space on the questionnaire for respondents to express anything they care to 169
    Once the questionnaire is developed and put into force, it cannot be changed 169
    Individual schools should not be allowed to circulate questionnaires similar to those being circulated by the school system 169
Drawing a Sample 169
Tabulating and Analyzing the Returns 170
Reporting Results 170
    What important points did the survey reveal? . . .170
    Are the totals significant? 170
    How can questions be combined to confirm trends? 170

Are results different than expected?	170
What survey method was used?	171
How were the questions prepared?	171
Who was the sponsor of the survey?	171
When did the survey take place?	171
Sample Questionnaire	172

13. How to Avoid Mistakes 175

Understand the Phrase "Decision-Making
Process" under School Based Management 175
Provide Adequate Training and Staff Development .. 176
Obtain Input from Stakeholders 176
Avoid Overuse of Vote-Taking 177
Clarify the Roles of Outside Consultants 178
Place a Reserve in the School Budget 178
Adhere to Parameters 179
Keep Parents Informed 180
Stay In Charge 180
Understand the Role of the Central Office 180
Apply Discretionary Powers Carefully 181
Keep Student Learning as the Highest Priority 181
Be Open-Minded 182
Use Delegation Properly 182
Be Wiling to Take Risks 183

14. DOs and DON'Ts 185

Appendix: Do You Have School Based Management? 199

Bibliography 203

Chapter 1

Why School Based Management?

There are about 15,500 public school districts in America, and only a small minority of these have implemented formal, advanced management decentralization. Nevertheless, there is great interest in and curiosity about the decentralization of school management, the most common form of which being referred to as "school based management." Hundreds of articles and a growing number of books have been written on the topic. An increasing number of school systems are experimenting with, and several state legislatures have mandated, some form of decentralized school management. A host of seminars and conferences have been held throughout the United States to learn more about the topic. We have, in fact, the emergence of a serious trend which is likely to be around for a long time.

Why will the interest in school based management be of long-term interest? First, the dissatisfaction with the current and conventional approach to education is intensifying in many communities. In such school systems, radical change is inevitable, and radical changes are not easily reversible. Second, if a successful transition to school based management is made, it is proof that a new and powerful constituency has developed for decentralized management. A successful school based management system is based upon the presence of majority support among parents, teachers, students, school administrators and school board members. Once parents, teachers, and principals get a taste of local control, they are very resistant to any attempt to take that control away for reconsolidation in the central office.

School based management is being experimented with because some people in the public education family *desire* to change. They know there is a better way to run a store and they are going to try. Many of these people in our public education family *believe* that school based management is the way to go, and their actions are simply following their beliefs. Who are these people among us who are pushing school based management?

- A small number of superintendents are actively providing leadership in the decentralization of school management. True, a few of these superintendents are habitual bandwagon passengers, but most of these professional educators truly believe that decentralization of management results not only in a more effective management organization, but better educational opportunities for children. These men and women actually believe that by "letting go" of power, they empower the school system generally. These men and women are risk takers, and as such, some will succeed and some will fail.

  It is understandable that some superintendents are reluctant to let go of their assigned powers. In the eyes of many school board members, an effective superintendent is one who takes charge and makes things happen over the opposition of others. In the eyes of such board members, a "good" superintendent is one that influences, controls, and manipulates others to achieve stated objectives. Is it any wonder that such superintendents might have difficulty letting go of their powers?

- Although their numbers are few, there are actually some school board members who believe at least in the theory of decentralized management. These people believe that some decisions should be left to the discretion of the local school, other decisions should be left to the central administration, while policy decisions should be left to the school board.

These few school board members are different from others in that they believe that a larger proportion of decisions should be left to the discretion of the local school community.

It is not easy for school board members to "let go." Many believe that power is a necessary tool in running the schools. Many believe in "top-down" management. Most are concerned with matters of fairness and equity, and view school based management as an invitation to inconsistency, discrimination, and inequity. Until convinced otherwise will most board members resist school based management. Changing this can only come with the education of an open mind. Therefore, no school board or school board members should support school based management until they are convinced that it has good potential for improving the schools.

- Some central office administrators want to decentralize management. This desire is less prevalent among central office administrators than among school principals. Central office administrators are accustomed to staff, budgets, rank, and clout. To some, decentralization means loss of these powers. On the other hand, a significant number of principals do favor school based management. They know that when enacted properly, school based management will offer them more opportunities to be professional leaders in their communities. I certainly don't want to imply that all principals support school based management. Some much prefer a highly centralized management structure within which principals are told what to do.

- There is considerable support from teachers for the local management of schools, particularly among teachers who have had experience with such a method. When done right, school based management gives teachers more influence in matters affecting their classroom work. These satisfied teachers talk to other teachers, and as a result the topic of school based management spreads to other school systems. True, not all teachers support this change. Some, as is the case on any faculty, prefer to be left alone.

- Under certain conditions, teacher unions favor school based management. If a union is convinced that collective bargaining contracts will not be violated, and that the union will have some influence in local management, the union is likely to provide support. It is management's job, however, to assure that school based management does not become another level of union negotiations, nor an opening to expand negotiable topics into the area of management rights, nor the cause of labor-management hostilities.

- Many credible, recognized scholars and professional consultants support school based management. When they speak and write, many listen and read. When such leading educators say school management should be decentralized, many among us take that seriously.

- A few school systems which have successfully decentralized stand as models for others interested in the move. The best example is the Edmonton, Alberta (Canada) public school system. It has the longest record of success (over ten years). The current superintendent of the system, Dr. Michael Strembitsky, originated the change and provides leadership for the effort to this day. Hundreds of visitors have examined the Edmonton schools and have come away convinced that it is a good system. Dr. Strembitsky not only teaches by modeling, but he is in great demand as a speaker and consultant in Canada, the United States, and abroad.

- Many examples exist in the private sector to support the concepts embodied in school based management. The best example is the Saturn automobile being manufactured by General Motors in Tennessee. This car has just recently come off the assembly line and is the result of a radical new management approach involving the management tactics of "ownership", team work, and collaboration—all elements found in school based management. The adoption of this new management plan by General Motors was the result of extensive study, and the corporation is staking its reputation on trying to prove that a new management system actually makes a better car. Many American business leaders, like those at General Motors, express their management views to public education officials. These business people have survived in a world of intense competition by satisfying their customers. When they speak, many in the public education establishment listen.

- Finally, parents increasingly are demanding a voice in the affairs of their local schools. The education address by President Bush on April 18, 1991, made it clear that school systems should open up to real parent involvement. One of the leading organizations for parent advocacy in the schools is the National Committee for Citizens in Education (Columbia, MD). I highly recommend this organization to school systems seeking a good training program for parents, leaders, students, and principals on making school based management work.

As a result of pressure to restructure public education, a number of state legislatures have passed laws requiring various forms of decentralized management. These laws are an indication that political forces are building for change. Unfortunately, the state laws enacted so far may do as much harm as good. Since many laws simply reflect the desires of special interest groups, laws mandating school based management are too often blatant attempts by special interest groups to get their way. In such cases, the student is often forgotten.

Hopefully, if further state legislation is needed to encourage school districts to decentralize, such laws will be general in nature, setting only broad guidelines for enhancing the powers of local school to respond to specific community needs. Overly specific laws defeat the whole concept of school based management in reducing the authority of local schools and school boards to make their own decisions.

Chapter 2

What Makes Good Schools?

It is true that increased financial support for education can contribute to better schools, particularly if the increased funds are based upon improvement in educational quality. But increased funds are not always available to the extent we would like. Therefore, we need to examine ways that schools can be improved with minimal reliance on additional funding.

Good schools are often the result of certain essential characteristics:

- Clarity of purpose
- Leadership
- Professionalism
- Lack of bureaucratic control
- Owned by stakeholders
- Effective use of resources
- Competition
- Choice

Clarity of Purpose

A good school has a clear purpose which is understood and supported by the principal, the staff, the students, the parents, and other school partners. This is why some private and parochial schools perform better than public schools. (This is not to suggest that all private and parochial schools are better than all public schools. Some private and parochial schools are better than some public schools, and some public schools are better than some private schools.) Many private and religious schools exist for a very clear reason. Their purpose may be to get their students in to the best colleges, to provide a military discipline, to develop excellence in the performing arts, or to instill a firm religious belief. In all such cases, the schools are committed to a clear purpose, supported by all participants.

Leadership

There is seldom a good school without good leadership. In most cases the term "leadership" refers to the quality of the school principal; however, leadership must exist in varying degrees among all members of the school partnership. In other words, the principal should not be the only competent leader. A principal (particularly in a large school) cannot accomplish the job of leadership alone. The principal must train others to be good leaders, too. Department heads, grade level chairpersons, PTA presidents, head custodians, committee chairpersons, etc., all have important leadership roles which need to be developed and supported by the principal. And school based management provides an ideal environment for leadership skills to flourish, in that this method of operating the schools gives freedom and encouragement for people to become their best.

The leadership skills needed by a principal to survive in a controlled bureaucratic setting are somewhat different from those skills needed by a principal in a school based management setting. In a controlled bureaucratic setting, principals are judged by their ability to follow rules, regulations and orders from above and to impress the important powers within that bureaucracy. Under decentralized management, there are fewer orders from above and the principal is more accountable to stakeholders in the school, that is, students, parents, and school employees.

This revised structure of management requires principals who are entrepreneurs, who are willing to take risks, and who are innovators, not those who are constrained by convention. The principals who are successful in a highly centralized mode of administration may not be the same ones who are successful under school based management. In hiring principals for schools that are site managed, superintendents should look for candidates who have the special qualifications that school based management requires.

Professionalism

A good school is one in which the entire staff is highly professional. This generally means that the staff's highest priority is the welfare of the client, that is, the student. It means that each staff member has a set of unique skills and is allowed to apply those skills with a reasonable degree of discretion. This concept of professionalism applies to all school building employees: the custodian, the secretary, the bus driver, and especially the "certificated" staff, that is, teachers and others who work directly with students. Although all staff members should be given both freedom and supervision in carrying out their duties, teachers need more leeway than others in implementing their daily classroom activities.

Professionalism thrives on school based management and school based management thrives on professionalism. Successful implementation requires teachers who can conduct their affairs responsibly, effectively, and free of constant supervision. Successful professionalism requires a management structure which allows teachers the needed freedom and encouragement to do their best while being true to themselves as individuals.

Lack of Bureaucratic Control

Good schools are free from excessive internal and external bureaucratic control. This means that good schools can neither be dictated from the superintendent's office nor from the principal's office. It means that each school is allowed reasonable freedom to operate in a manner which is uniquely beneficial to the individual school community. The more the central office tries to direct every aspect of the local school operation, the greater is the risk that maximum performance will not be obtained from the staff. And, carried to an extreme, excessive rules and regulations can actually impede school improvement.

School based management cannot succeed under highly centralized administration, and highly centralized administration cannot succeed where there is real school based management. This is not to suggest, however, that some school system operations (e.g., student transportation) should not be administered centrally. It does suggest, though, that the central office should carry out its executive function in a manner which allows each school to perform at its best. This clearly implies a process of "letting go" of certain central powers and transferring those powers (e.g., selection of school supplies) to the local school.

Owned by Stakeholders

Good schools are "owned" by the stakeholders. Although the school board, the superintendent, and the central office staff are all stakeholders in the school system, the real stakeholders are at the school level. They are the students themselves whose lives are directly influenced by their school experiences. They are the teachers who must teach the students each day. They are the parents who send their children to the schools and who want the best for them. They are the principals who are those held most accountable for the success or failure of the school. These are the key people to whom the central office should defer to build strong schools.

When people are allowed to make decisions and are held accountable for those decisions, they tend to be much more analytical and responsible in making those decisions and will strive to make those decisions work. However, when these same people are told what to do (particularly in areas where they have expertise and where they have a stake), they often take less responsibility for such decisions and provide less effort to make such decisions work. When teachers, students, parents and principals feel they "own" their schools, benefit from their wise decisions, and suffer from their unwise decisions, there is great potential to build a good school.

Effective Use of Resources

Schools can be improved by making better use of the funds already available. There is no causal relationship between increased expenditures for education and the quality of education. But even if such a relationship did exist, the funds are not forthcoming.

One of the advantages of school based management is that it makes better use of available funds. Under a highly centralized system of management, money is "free". The total school system budget is held by the central office and the schools go hat in hand to get what they can. And usually they ask for more than they need because the know they will not get everything they ask for, regardless of the amount. Such a system is ripe for abuse and misuse of funds. As long as funds come from the central office, the local schools (where most of the money is spent) have limited accountability for how funds are spent.

Under school based management, the largest share of the entire school system budget is allocated to the schools in a lump sum. Under this system, there is no more "free" money in the central office. The only funds left in the central office are the limited funds necessary to run central operations. By transferring most of the school system budget to the local schools, the accountability for the use of those funds is increased. Also, by transferring funds to the schools, each school has a greater opportunity to use those limited funds effectively. This belief is based upon the concept that stakeholders in the local school have the most to lose or gain by prudent use of their resources.

Competition

In a free market system, providers compete with each other to see who can serve the consumer best. Those who fail to serve the customer go out of business as they should. Those who serve the customer will prosper as they should. This competition among providers is what makes the free market system superior to all other systems in serving the customer. The combined incentives of fear of failure and hope of prosperity are what drive superior American businesses. Without competition, there is reduced incentive to serve the customer or to improve.

Diversity among schools in a given school system is a strong sign that school based management is at work. Just as free competition can serve the customer best in the private sector, so can competition serve the customer better in the public school sector. Although school based management will not bring free market competition to elementary and secondary education, it has the potential for allowing schools to be different and for allowing bad schools to lose student customers and good schools to gain student customers.

Choice

But diversity and competition can have limited value unless students are allowed to choose the school they attend. Ideally, this choice should extend to the choice of a private school, but that is not likely in the near future. The next best option is to extend choice to any public school.

Advocates of choice maintain that the obvious advantages of choice are:

- The continued enrollment of students in a school is somewhat dependent upon the quality of that school. If a school is unacceptable to students (and parents), some will chose to attend a more acceptable school. The availability and exercise of such choice puts pressure on each school to perform in a manner acceptable to its clientele.

- When students are forced to attend a specific school, they have no "ownership" in that decision. As a result, many students develop negative attitudes toward their school which interfere with their learning and adjustment. Choice allows students and parents to accept accountability for their decision. Although choice does not guarantee that all schools will get better or guarantee that all students will be satisfied with their educational experiences, choice improves the possibility for such developments.

School based management is an ideal public school management model within which to allow choice. School based management brings about diversity among the schools. Diversity implies that students should have a choice, and choice sets into motion the advantages of competition.

Is School Based Management the Answer?

In August of 1990, the Rand Corporation published a study entitled "High Schools with Character". The study was a successful attempt to gain insight into what factors create an effective high school. The in-depth study was based upon an analysis of high schools in New York City and Washington. In summary, the report found that successful high schools have clear, simple, and understandable missions focused on student learning and attitudes, as well as organizational structures which enable those schools to initiate actions and solve problems.

Examples of such successful schools were Catholic high schools and "special interest" public schools. The Catholic high schools achieved this distinction despite lower teacher salaries than those received by public school teachers, despite larger class sizes, despite the fact that many of the teachers are not "certified," and despite a per pupil financial expenditure lower than that in the public schools. They achieved their success because they were "focused" in their mission, organization and performance. The public schools which achieved a similar mark of success were "special-interest" schools which had a similar focus in their functioning.

By contrast, the report found that most comprehensive high schools (which includes most of the high schools in the nation) are ineffective because they are nothing more than "franchises" following rules issued from a distant central office. Such schools are not focused, and therefore diffuse their effectiveness.

While many educational leaders and scholars are turning to school based management and choice as significant contributors to improved student learning and behavior, the Rand study argues that such reforms, although good, are not sufficient. School based management as practiced in most places, according to the report, "promises to accomplish little beyond transferring the politics of interest groups negotiation from the school district to the school building." Concerning the concept that the freedom for parents and students to choose will create a consumer demand and thereby improve the schools through competition, the report contends, "Like money in the hands of consumers, choice creates the opportunity for people to buy what they want if they can find it. But purchasing power has little meaning if there are no attractive goods to choose. Demand alone cannot produce good inner-city schools."

Is the Rand report correct in its conclusion? Yes, to a degree. School based management, although a potentially good way of managing the public schools, cannot succeed fully without the characteristics of a "focused" school. Choice, although also a potentially good option for parents and students, cannot succeed fully without the diversity that springs from "focused" schools. However, choice and school based management can help unfocused schools become "focused". Proper school based management allows schools to be different. Different schools bring meaning to choice, and choice brings competition. And, competition means schools must satisfy the customer in order to survive.

In summary, school based management, choice, and focused school operation are the basic triad for improved student learning. They are not competing components, but should complement and supplement each other. To the extent that this happens, schools should improve.

What are the principal characteristics of "focused" schools and "zoned" schools? According to the Rand Report:

1. Focused schools are free of external and internal barriers to invention and initiative.

   Zoned schools have both external and internal barriers to invention and initiative.

2. Focused schools have clear, uncomplicated missions centered on the ways the students will benefit and change in response to those experiences.

   Zoned schools have confused and complicated missions which are more institutional and political, with less emphasis upon student benefits.

3. Focused schools are strong organizations able to initiate action to pursue their missions, to sustain themselves over time, and to manage their external relationships.

   Zoned schools have less ability to initiate action at the school level, require external energy to sustain programs, and are often at the mercy of external political events.

4. Focused schools concentrate on student outcomes to the virtual exclusion of all other matters.

   Zoned schools concentrate primarily on delivering programs and following procedures.

5. Focused schools have strong social contracts that communicate the reciprocal responsibilities of administrators, students, and teachers and establish the benefits that each can derive from fulfilling the contract faithfully.

   Zoned schools try whenever possible to let staff and students define their own roles in the school.

6. Focused schools have a strong commitment to parenting, acting aggressively to mold student attitudes and values.

   Zoned schools see themselves primarily as transmitters of information and imparters of skills.

7. Focused schools have curricula that draw all students toward learning certain core skills and perspectives.

   Zoned schools distinguish sharply among students in terms of ability and preference and offer profoundly different curricula to different groups.

8. Focused schools operate as problem-solving organizations, taking the initiative to change their programs in response to emerging needs.

   Zoned schools have external and rigid internal divisions of labor which constrain the problem-solving process.

9. Focused schools sustain their own organizational character, both by attracting staff members who accept the school's premises and by socializing new staff members.

   Zoned schools have little capacity to select staff or influence the attitudes or behavior of new staff members.

10. Focused schools consider themselves accountable to the people who depend on their performance—parents, students, neighborhood and parish groups, financial supporters, and admirers elsewhere in the community.

    Zoned schools answer primarily to bureaucratic superiors, including outside rule-making, auditing, and assessment organizations.

In short, *focused schools are designed to influence and change students; zoned schools are designed to administer programs and deliver services.* School based management is highly compatible with the concept of focused schools.

Chapter 3
School Based Management Defined

SCHOOL BASED MANAGEMENT* is a research based, committed, structured, and decentralized method of operating the school district within understood parameters and staff roles to maximize resource effectiveness by transferring the preponderant share of the entire school system's budget, along with corresponding decision-making power, to the local schools on an equitable lump-sum basis, based upon a differentiated per pupil allocation to be spent irrespective of source in the best interests of the students in those schools according to a creative local school plan and local school budget developed by the principal collaboratively with trained staff, parents and students as stakeholders, and approved by the superintendent; such plans being designed to achieve approved goals of improving education by placing accountability at the individual school, and evaluated more by results than by methodology.

Within this complex definition there are thirteen major topic areas that encapsulate the essential elements necessary for an advanced form of school based management. Although there are some school districts which appear to be practicing various forms of school based management, few school districts fit the demanding definition articulated here. Each of these major topic areas

---

* "School based management" and "decentralized management" are used interchangeably in this book.

will be discussed as currently being practiced under a comprehensive and advanced form of decentralized management.

Commitment Is Needed

When a school district restructures from a highly centralized form of management to a decentralized one, as in the case of school based management, there are drastic changes in the procedures by which the school district is operated, and there are drastic changes in the roles of people and offices within the organization. These changes create uncertainty and may give rise to confusion and resistance. To reduce the risk of a failed transition, all key players—the school board members, the superintendent, central office administrators, principals, teachers and other employees, students, and parents—need to be firmly committed to the idea of decentralization as set out in school based management, regardless of where within the school system the idea originates.

Understandably, the support of the local school board is a requirement. Although school based management is largely an executive and administrative function, and not a responsibility of the governing body (the school board), the school board must understand and support whatever system the chief executive officer (the superintendent) employs to run the school district. Lacking this support and understanding, otherwise avoidable conflicts are bound to arise. School based management cannot succeed if the school board does not grasp and support the concept of decentralization or "letting go." School board intrusion into the day-to-day operation of the schools under any structure of administration is bad, but such intrusion completely undermines school based management. If a board insists on prohibiting reasonable school based activities, or persists in interfering with approved and legitimate school based decisions, school based management cannot succeed. Decentralized administration requires that the school board clearly understand the limits of its own role. There is no quicker way to destroy school based management than for the school board to interfere with the legitimate autonomy of the stakeholders within the individual schools.

Equal in importance to the role of the school board, is the commitment of the superintendent to decentralized management. Even if the school board is knowledgeable and supportive of school based management, the system cannot function without the superintendent's full loyalty to both the idea and its application. Unless the superintendent truly believes that school based management is the best management system to improve education, and is willing to stake his or her job on its success, the superintendent should not adopt such a system. Any less of a commitment by the chief executive officer of the school district will threaten success. Furthermore, the superintendent must demonstrate commitment to the school based management to all parties by specific actions designed to implement the system. To do otherwise will call into question the superintendent's true support, set a bad example for other key players, and cause unneeded confusion.

When a school district converts from centralized to decentralized management, some resistance can be expected from "entrenched" central office administrators, particularly in large school districts where some administrators possess considerable power. To these veteran administrators, school based management is a threat, in that power and funds move from the central office to the field. For an administrator long accustomed to the power that title, money, and staff bring, it should not be a surprise to discover that decentralization is not always a welcome change.

Recognizing this fact, which is inevitable to some degree in all cases of transition, it is the clear responsibility of the superintendent to minimize any such resistance. Exactly how the superintendent does this, however, will vary from situation to situation. In any case the superintendent can make it clear in many ways that he is determined that school based management will succeed and that all employees are expected to diligently support the program.

As a general rule, once they understand school based management (as defined at the beginning of this chapter), principals, teachers, students, and parents generally will support it, because school based management has improved the lot of these stakeholders. Under decentralization (if done properly) the principal has an enhanced opportunity to be a better educational leader. The teachers receive an opportunity that they have demanded for decades—to influence in a meaningful way the affairs which affect their work in the classroom. Not surprisingly, parents generally support school based management more than a centralized system of management because they, too, have increased influence in and ownership of the local school. And, if carried out properly, the students are loyal to decentralized management because they share, along with other stakeholders, an ownership in their own education.

School Based Management Is a Structured Decentralized Method of Operating the School System

School based management is a carefully designed and organized management system based on administrative decentralization as a viable management step toward initiative for better education. *Such a structured system has its own unique in-service and staff development program, a tailor-made budget program and evaluation model, clear parameters, a very creative equity guarantee for students, a process for making decisions, a method for taking actions based on goals, a way to use a local school plan and budget to achieve these goals, a method to involve faculty, parents, and students meaningfully, and a means of achieving accountability based upon results.* In other words, school based management, as discussed in this chapter, is a dynamic way of managing a school system with its own methods, processes, techniques, and concepts.

School Based Management Operates within Understood Parameters

As discussed previously, school based management is an effectively structured way of improving education and of making better use of resources. It is not a license for local schools to do anything they wish. Even under an advanced form of decentralized management, there are many limitations upon the discretion of the local school. For example, all laws dealing with the operation of public schools must be observed. All state regulations governing the public schools must be obeyed, unless a waiver is approved. School accreditation standards must be followed, if schools are to be accredited. Local school board policy remains in force, unless the board modifies or rescinds its own policies to allow for some action properly called for and approved under school based management. All regulations set out by the superintendent continue in force until such regulations are changed by the superintendent to permit some worthwhile school based activity. In other words, *each school operates according to "business as usual" until the school has an approved school plan (and funds) to do otherwise.*

Existing contracts are also parameters. Forty-two states have laws governing collective bargaining for teachers. As a result, thousands of school districts have labor contracts in force. In most instances, these contracts are binding and therefore must be considered when converting to school based management. To what extent these labor contracts restrict educational improvement through decentralization is a question which remains unanswered.

Some school districts may be tempted to make a list of parameters before entering into school based management, to provide responsible "control" over the schools. The problem with this approach, however, is two-fold. First, once such a list is started, it becomes an endless process, degenerating into useless quibbling. Second, the making of such a (long) list sends out the wrong signal for successful school based management. It is not wise to embark upon decentralized management, based upon initiative at the individual school, by dictating all the things that cannot be done. This is an effective way to destroy initiative. Naturally, if there are activities under which no conditions will be permitted as a school based function (e.g., student bus transportation), then these few parameters can be announced and explained before schools write their school plans. But, as stated previously, the most effective way to deal with parameters is to operate the school system on a "business as usual" basis until to do otherwise has been approved in the local school plan.

All Players Must Understand Their Roles

As is true in any management system, success depends on all participants knowing their roles and responsibilities. Anything less results in inaction, duplication, conflicts, and in general, reduced effectiveness. This rule is especially true of school based management, in which so many players are allowed into the game. Without a clear understanding of who does what, there can be chaos. The school board must understand its policymaking and oversight roles and stay out of administrative matters. The superintendent, under school based management, continues to function as the chief executive officer, but must carry out duties within the limits of democratic decentralization. Specifically, the superintendent must learn to trust local school stakeholders by "letting go." Under school based management, many central office supervisors must learn to become "consultants" rather than "supervisors." Under advanced school based management, the local schools make decisions regarding instructional and management matters (within parameters), and it is the function of the central office staff to consult with and assist the local school in this endeavor.

At the local school level, decentralized management places new responsibilities on teachers, students, and parents, as well as the school principal. Furthermore, all of these people at the school level must learn to work together.

After all roles and responsibilities for school based management have been clearly defined, the school district should put in writing, for official use, a "roles and responsibilities" statement for each job classification, such as assistant superintendent, director, supervisor, principal, teacher, etc. This will greatly help in achieving educational aims.

Maximized Resource Effectiveness

Although the major purpose of school based management is to improve education in the public schools by laying out the structure to encourage creativity and innovation, another purpose is to make better use of the limited resources available. School based management works from the premise that resources are used best at the level where they are consumed, assuming accountability is attached to the use of those resources. Under centralized budgeting and management, money is "free" to the schools; the central office owns the money and gives it to the school as the central office sees fit. The local schools do not own any money, so they can afford not to make the best use of such money, since someone else is paying. Under decentralized management and budgeting, the local schools own the lion's share of the entire school system budget and are held accountable (based upon specific results) for the money they spend. Experience has proven that once the local school becomes the owner of dollars, the principal, teachers, parents, and students become much more responsible in the use of those dollars.

One example from the Prince William County experience can serve as an illustration of how school based management conserves the school district resources. Under the previous centralized system of administration, allotments for textbooks were made centrally. Thus, when a school could justify a greater need (as they often did), it was the expected responsibility of the central office to provide funds for the "needed" textbooks. Now, under school based management, limited funds for textbooks are included in the individual school's total allocation, so school principals can no longer go to the textbook office to beg for additional funds. As a result, schools are much more protective of their textbooks; fewer books are damaged or lost. The better a school takes care of its textbooks, the more money becomes available for other purposes. Many other examples of the results from school based management can be given.

The Preponderant Share of the Budget Must Be Transferred to the Schools

Research, experience, and observation of a large number of school districts which claim to be on school based management indicate that *there is a direct correlation between the amount of money transferred to the control of local schools and the extent to which there is true management at the school level.* There is no better test of the commitment to school based management than the amount of money transferred from the central office to the individual schools. Many school districts claim to be following school based management practices, when in fact budget control remains in the central office. For a school district to be fully committed to the concept of school based management, at least 75% of the entire school system's operating budget should be spent by the local schools. By transferring the bulk of the district's funds and decision-making responsibilities to the schools, the local school principal is empowered to manage the school and to be held accountable for a quality program. Under this arrangement, the principal has the ability to hire all employees; purchase all supplies, furniture, and equipment needed by the school; structure the organization of the school; and implement a quality education program—all within known parameters. (Incidentally, when this takes place, salaries should be adjusted upward for principals to attract, retain, and reward the holders of such important positions.)

Appropriate Decision-Making Power Must Accompany the Transfer of Funds

The transfer of funds away from the central bureaucracy is a painful process for those on the "losing" side. This pain is doubled when decision-making power is transferred at the same time. For example, when the supervisor of media and library services in the central office has all funds for library books and related materials transferred to the schools, the power to purchase those books and related materials is also transferred to the principal. This transfer is necessary under school based management where the principal is held accountable for the library and media program in the local school. With money in hand and power to spend it, the principal truly can be held accountable for the quality of that program. If principals are to be held accountable for the quality of the math program in their schools, they must be given the money to hire math teachers, the power to direct those teachers, the money to purchase supplies and equipment, and the power to make such purchases. Under this arrangement, most of the central office supervisors and administrators become "consultants" to principals and are pledged to give assistance, rather than direction. Under school based management, only one person gives direction to the principal, and that is the principal's boss; and each principal must be restricted to just one boss.

Those who are inexperienced with school based management often claim that the approach overwhelms the principal with non-instructional and non-educational management duties. While it is true that school based management broadens the management scope of the principal, the power of the principal to make all things in the school work together for improved education is strengthened. If the central office has the funds for grass cutting at the schools and is accountable for cutting grass at the schools, there is a distinct possibility that the grass will be cut at a time which the local school finds objectionable. On the other hand, if the local school is held accountable for grass cutting and has the funds to accomplish this task, then the principal has control over activities which have indirect impact on the school environment.

Interviews of principals who have served under both a centralized and a decentralized system of management have uncovered none who would return to centralized management. If principals are the best judge of what is going on in their schools, then we must trust their opinion about the viability of school based management.

Funds Must Be Allocated Equitably on a Differentiated Per Pupil Allocation

The more money that is transferred to the schools from the central office, the more care must be taken to assure that the money is allocated to the schools on an equitable basis. For example, if there are two elementary schools, both with 500 students, chances are it would not be equitable to allocate the same amount of money to both schools. One school might have 75 handicapped students requiring an average expenditure of $6,000 each, while the other school might have only 25 handicapped students. One school might have more gifted students than the other, and one school might have more economically disadvantaged students than the other. In other words, even though two schools may have the same number of students, each school has different needs based on the makeup of students enrolled in that school. Therefore, it is necessary to determine the cost of the various categories of students, such as those in the special education and gifted programs, those who are economically disadvantaged, etc. Also, the cost of educating students varies from grade level to grade level. High school students on the average cost more to educate than middle school students, and middle school students on the average cost more to educate than elementary students.

Under the school based management model being described here, *the money follows the student*. A trainable mentally retarded student might be assigned $10,000, while a "regular" third grader might be assigned $3,000. When the amount of money assigned to each student in his assigned category is added together, the principal has a total (lump sum) figure upon which to prepare a school plan and develop a school budget. For example, in an elementary school of 500 students, the total amount of money to which that school is entitled might be $2 million. This money is allocated to the school in a *lump sum*. Where the money comes from is irrelevant to the school. What is important is that the school has a lump sum of $2 million to hire teachers, purchase supplies and equipment, and take whatever other action is appropriate within approved parameters and affordable limits to deliver a quality educational program at that school.

In summary, there is a link between the portion of the school district's budget assigned to the school and the commitment to school based management. Also, the hallmark of good school based management is an allocation made to the school in a lump sum, giving the school the freedom to spend that money according to its approved school plan. Finally, the way to assure an equitable education for each child is to arrange all school allocations on a differentiated per pupil basis. A school district that violates any of these three rules has a questionable school based management program.

Funds Must Be Spent According to the Best Interests of Students as Determined by an Individual School Plan and Individual School Budget

If the individual schools are to spend the bulk of the school district's budget, then spending must be carried out according to individual school plans which have been collaboratively developed and approved by the superintendent. All of the school plans should be in a practical format which can be understood by the average adult. However, this format should be consistent among the schools; otherwise, it becomes an unmanageable task for the superintendent (and his staff) to review and approve such plans. Whatever plan format is used, it should be the result of open minded collaboration between the schools and the superintendent.

Each annual school plan should explain clearly what the school intends to do for the coming school year, and should be accompanied by a school budget showing how the activities called for in the plan will be paid for. (The funds for this budget come from the lump sum allocation to the school based on a differentiated per pupil allocation.) The school plan should not go into every operational detail of the school, but should concentrate on the major thrusts of the school. In most cases, the school plan should be divided into sections with each section addressing a different goal or objective. Among the goals will be those mandated by the school board or the superintendent, while others will be set within the individual school. For example, one goal section of the plan might describe how the school intends to carry out the school board goal to improve reading skills and comprehension at the elementary school level. Another goal section might be devoted to a locally set objective to beautify the front entrance of the school.

Each goal in the school plan should be developed in a consistent manner. One approach is a clear statement of the goal, followed by a brief statement of the problem or problems which need to be overcome in order to achieve that goal. Then attention needs to be given to the strategies and tactics to be used to achieve the goal. This section should include how personnel will be used, what non-personnel resources will be employed, a calendar of activities, and any other information needed to describe how the objective will be achieved. For each goal, there must be a method of evaluating whether or not acceptable progress was made on that particular objective. This evaluation statement becomes an important factor in the principal's own evaluation at the end of the school year.

Just as the school plan should be a clear verbal explanation of the school budget, the school budget should be a clear financial statement of the school plan. Although there are many ways to display a school budget, the school district should agree to one format to be used by all schools. Regardless of the format, however, it should be easy to read, to implement, and to transfer funds for good reason. As far as possible, transfer of funds at the local school level should be at the discretion of the principal, but should be monitored by his supervisor. Naturally, any legal requirements regarding transfer of funds or wise accounting practices must be observed.

School Plans and Budgets Should Result from Collaboration among Parents, Faculty, Students, and the Principal

An infallible and indispensable telltale sign of real school based management is the presence of meaningful collaboration in the development of the school plan and its accompanying annual school budget. When practicing decentralized management, each school should be required to have in place a functioning collaboration process which involves faculty, parents, students, and the principal. How this process is organized should vary somewhat among the schools. For example, collaboration among stakeholders at a large high school calls for a structure different than that at a small elementary school.

Regardless of variations in collaboration plans, however, all such plans should share certain common elements. For example, each collaboration plan must include the regular involvement of representatives of teachers selected by teachers, representatives of parents selected by parents, and representatives of students selected by students. These people must play the key roles in developing the school plan and budget. And, the principal should not dominate the collaborative process. Finally, there should be provision to assure that the collaboration process is not restricted to the same persons over a protracted period of time. Although there are other guidelines for making the collaboration process successful, these suggestions are the most important.

Special attention should be given to the role of the principal in the collaboration process. As a general rule, school principals are held accountable for what goes on in the school. It is the principal who is terminated when something serious goes wrong. It is the principal who is turned to when directives are issued by the superintendent. The local school site committee is not held accountable for the success or the failure of the school. This is not to suggest that such committees are titular in nature. For school based management to work properly, there must be a place in the system of collaboration which results in sound advice which the principal should follow in most cases. And, if a proper collaboration system is in place, the principal will get good advice. The principal's failure to follow such good advice would be the first step toward finding a new principal. The issue of who runs the school is a non-issue. *The principal runs the school under the close scrutiny and advice of faculty, parents, and students, but under the supervision of the superintendent.*

Thorough Preparation Is Essential

When a school district has operated under highly centralized management for many years, the people in that system—the school board, the administrators, the teachers, and the parents—have learned to behave accordingly. When such a system converts to decentralization based upon collaboration, new rules and responsibilities are created. Therefore, all parts must be helped to succeed within the new way of doing business. Administrators must provide the school board with sessions on how school based management works and how the new process will affect the school board. For example, under school based management, the school board should be willing to give individual schools more freedom to handle their own affairs. Also, the school board should be willing to allow schools to vary the ways in which they carry out their responsibilities.

Central office administrators need to understand their new "consultation" role and should be helped to accept and support the expanded role of the principal. Teachers need in-service programs on their new collaboration role. They need training in consensus building, resolving conflict, team-building, writing a school plan, and developing a school budget. Similarly, parents and students need training in how to function in the collaborative process.

Of greatest importance is the training provided for the principal. As stated earlier, the principal is held accountable for the training of the staff, the parents, and the students. Therefore, the principal should be given special consideration in the staff development program for school based management. The training should include: how to write a school plan, how to prepare a school budget, how to coordinate collaboration, how to carry out purchasing responsibilities, how to utilize the allocation formula, how to develop evaluation processes for the school plan, how to conduct a needs assessment, and how to carry out non-instructional and non-educational management functions. Since the principal is held accountable for the success and stability of the school, he or she is entitled to premium training.

The Superintendent Must Approve All School Plans and Budgets

As school plans are being developed, some schools may ask for waivers from certain school board policies and certain administrative regulations. In such a case, the request is reviewed while the plan is being formulated. If possible, the superintendent should approve or reject any changes before the plan is finalized, so that difficult issues are resolved promptly.

The superintendent should keep the school board informed of all important activities related to school based management and should provide the board with a copy of each school plan. However, the board should not put itself in the role of approving individual school plans. This responsibility would burden the board unnecessarily, put the board in the position of administering the schools, and take administrative discretion away from the schools.

School Plans Should Be Designed to Carry Out Goals of Improved Education

Under school based management, goals come from several sources: the school board has a right and obligation to set long-range goals (e.g., to install air-conditioning in schools over a period of years), the superintendent may set goals (e.g., to have all principals complete a prescribed training program), central office administrators may set goals for their offices (e.g., to institute an electronic mail system), and individual schools must establish their own individual goals (e.g., to beautify the school's front entrance).

All of these goals, however, should be based on an overriding mission of the school system, a mission that is supported by all those in the school system family. For example, a school district might decide that its most important mission is: **To provide an educational program that promotes the belief that all students can learn and achieve at their highest potential.**

Given this as the official mission statement of the school system, then all other goals and objectives should support this mission.

Evaluation Should Be on Results—Not Methodology

As stated earlier, the purpose of school based management is to improve education by promoting creativity and innovation and to use the limited resources available in better ways. The goal of "improved education" can be defined in many different ways, but whatever definition is assigned to "improved education," results, not methodology, should be considered in determining whether education has been improved under school based management.

If a school board decides that it wants to improve the "academic performance" of students as measured by certain tests, the superintendent should devise a means of showing the board what progress students are making year by year on these tests. That is a results-oriented evaluation! Since individual schools are evaluated on the results their students achieve on these tests, individual schools likely would include strategies to improve test scores.

There are many other results that the board or the superintendent might look for under school based management: number of students on the honor roll, scores on college entrance examinations, the number of Merit finalists and semi-finalists, student attendance, student retention, Advanced Placement scores and enrollments, drop-outs, and student suspensions.

One of the best ways to evaluate school based management is to survey practitioners and customers. The superintendent should develop a series of survey questionnaires which are distributed annually (near the end of the school year) to parents, students, teachers, administrators, and all other employees. These questionnaires should be ready at the outset of school based management and should remain basically unchanged over the years. The surveys should be developed collaboratively, but an expert should supervise development, sampling, and interpretation.

Such surveys are designed to discover if the stakeholders in the public school system are satisfied. By asking similar questions of teachers, parents, employees, and students, the superintendent can learn a great deal about how the schools are doing individually and as a system. The results of the surveys are tabulated, analyzed, and compared with results from previous years. A comparison of each year's results reveals the degree of support for future strategies to improve the schools.

Chapter 4

Pros and Cons

There Are Many Advantages to School Based Management

There is no justification for converting from a centralized form of administration to a decentralized one if there is no advantage in the change. The experience of the limited number of school districts that have embraced school based management, and a review of applicable literature, reveal a number of advantages which make decentralization superior to centralization.

Greater commitment by staff to decisions

Under school based management teachers and other staff members play an active part in decisions made at the school level. When teachers are a part of the decision-making process, there is good likelihood that they will support those decisions which they have helped make. If the principal makes decisions unilaterally, there is good likelihood that teachers will show less support for decisions in which they have had no part. With "ownership" in decisions comes commitment; with commitment comes improved quality of work. A school district can make a giant leap toward improved education if it can find a way to increase the commitment of employees to those decisions which must be made to run the schools. Collaborative decision making is one way to do it.

Greater support for how funds are spent

One of the purposes of school based management is to make the best use of the limited funds available to the school system. If all of the school system's budget is controlled by the central office, teachers and principals have diminished incentive to conserve. As far as the school staff is concerned, the money and supplies from the central office are "free," so they may as well ask for as much as they can. Under such financial control, the central office is a ready-made target to blame for anything that isn't right. Also, when the central office controls the purse strings, there is always the suspicion that there is pool of hidden money there. Such suspicion weakens the fabric of trust needed in all successful organizations.

However, when the largest share of the entire school system budget is transferred to the individual schools to be spent according to budgets devised in the schools (with the help of teachers), teachers are more likely to accept responsibility for the financial decisions for the school. Also, it should be kept in mind that under the school based management model described in this book, there are *no* spare funds left in the central office for use by local schools, as the central office controls only the amounts necessary to run their offices. When teachers understand that the schools have all of the money there is, they become more protective of the money provided to their school.

Increased professional growth

When teachers and principals are given more opportunity to run the schools, they are forced to reckon with a host of responsibilities previously handled by the central office. They must become familiar with the budget process, learn about purchasing, and generally become more accountable. They need to learn how to function in the school in a collaborative manner. In-service programs must be completed on team-building, conflict resolution, and problem-solving. All of these new-found challenges create great opportunity for intensified professional growth. Under school site management, teachers no longer are "just teachers"; they are members of the school team. This new role requires greater expertise and responsibilities.

Improvement in morale

With decentralization comes "ownership" by parents, students, and teachers; and, as owners, their views are sought, considered, and weighed heavily. Research studies conclude consistently that when employees are involved meaningfully in the operation of their organization, their attitude toward the employer is improved; and such an improvement in attitude usually results in better job performance.

The school board and public have a better view of spending

Most school system budgets are "program" budgets, which display the amount of money set aside for certain "programs" like personnel, maintenance, textbooks, utilities, supplies, transportation, etc. Such program budgets, however, seldom clearly show how much money is actually being spent on behalf of the individual school. This program approach to budgeting has several problems associated with it. First, individual schools feel only limited accountability for funds spent on their behalf, since these funds come from program budgets outside the control of the school. Second, the program budget holder is seldom held fully accountable for the outcome for which the budget has been appropriated. For example, the math supervisor, although the holder of a large math budget, cannot be held fully accountable for the success of the math program. Third, program budgets fail to provide a completely fair distribution of funds to the schools. Some schools get under-funded, while others are over-funded.

Under school site budgeting, the school board (and anyone else who is interested) can see clearly exactly how much money goes to each school and to each budget holder in the central office. Furthermore, the board can look at each individual school budget and see exactly how funds are being spent in that school. The same is true for each central office "program" budget, which is displayed in a manner making interpretation relative easy.

More effective spending of limited funds

When teachers realize that the schools have the largest share of the total school system budget and that there is no more money anywhere else for the schools, teachers tend to become more prudent in their financial decisions. It's one thing to spend "free" money (from the central office); but it's quite a different matter to spend one's own money. When teachers understand that they have significant control over how "their" money is spent, they will try to make every dollar count. For example, under school based budgeting, teachers are more likely to share to stretch the limited dollars. They share supplies, and equipment is made to do double duty. In this way, money is saved and can be applied to spending which otherwise would not have been possible. It is gratifying to see how innovative and protective teachers become when they take ownership of the school budget.

Educational equity is maximized

Dispersing the bulk of the school system budget to the individual schools on a differentiated per pupil basis assures that all schools and students get their equitable share of the total resources of the school system. Different groups of students receive different, but equitable, allocations depending upon their needs. For example, different amounts are provided for elementary, middle school, and high school students because of differing costs of education among these three levels. Along the same lines, educable mentally retarded students receive significantly more financial support than gifted students, because the former require more support than the latter. Under this "student based" budgeting procedure, discussed further elsewhere in this book, all students receive their fair and equitable share of educational support.

"Student based" budgeting is adaptable to vouchers and tuition credits

The American (public) school system is a monolithic, monopolistic institution trying to serve the educational needs of a free, pluralistic society. This is a difficult task. Although school based management will help bring about diversity through competition and community ownership (particularly if "school choice" is available), it will not give certain parents the educational options they want and need, such as those provided by vouchers and tuition credits. However, the "student based" budgeting aspect of school based management does provide a ready-made basis for determining appropriate amounts of money for each student taking advantage of vouchers or tuition credits.

School based management sets a good model for students

Under the traditional centralized school system administration, educational stakeholders have a limited voice in matters which affect them. Too often these stakeholders are told what and how to do things, and what is good for them. If we hope to help young people become independent and self-reliant adults, the schools must operate in a way which allows teachers and students to take responsibility for the educational process. School based management does just that. It practices what it preaches, and teachers, parents, and students are the beneficiaries of the process.

More leadership opportunity is provided for principals

Decentralization of management initially creates a degree of anxiety for some principals (although some can't wait to get started). They are uncertain how they will find time to carry out the additional work which they believe (wrongly) that the introduction of school site management will create. They believe (rightly) that school based management will increase accountability. And, they are concerned about unfamiliar budget responsibilities. All of these concerns are common at the outset, but the principals come to view the concerns as opportunities for professional growth.

The "extra work" disappears soon after principals learn how to handle their new responsibilities. They learn how to work smarter—not harder. They also find that increased control over the management of the school means better control over the principal's own workload, with delegation and budget control being the magic keys to a more effective workday for the principal. The increased accountability brings with it increased power for success, and success brings recognition and credit. While it is true that the principal must know how to manage a budget, this is preferable to having others manage that budget.

The school becomes more responsive to the community

Each school community is different from others, and has different educational needs. If a school system has a highly centralized bureaucracy, these individual school differences and needs are not adequately met, since the organization is unresponsive. Under decentralization, the school family, composed of students, teachers, and parents, writes its own annual school plan and develops its own annual school budget, forcing the school to respond to the educational needs of the students in that school community. The degree to which a school serves the educational needs of its community is an important hallmark of the school's effectiveness. School based management provides the means for keeping the local school in touch with its local community.

Teachers are empowered for enhanced student learning

Some teacher union leaders think the chief advantage of school based management is that teachers become "empowered". Teacher union actions and publications show that teacher self-interest is the highest priority of the unions. After all, this is what unions are supposed to do. But, this interpretation of "teacher empowerment" is antithetical to effective school based management. If decentralization is simply a transfer of raw power from one group to another, then nothing will change for the better. One set of problems will be replaced by another.

Teacher empowerment under enlightened decentralization means providing teachers with opportunities to affect the quality of student learning. It means providing a management structure so that teachers can give (and *want* to give) their best to the students. Union demands for teacher majorities on site committees mean union control, not improvement of student learning. The same is true of union demands that place teacher working conditions above student learning conditions. In these cases, labor relations, rather than academic needs determine the success of school based management. If teachers allow their unions to make "teacher power" the issue rather than student welfare, decentralization will not succeed.

Educational concerns take highest priority

Bureaucratic matters are more likely to be of concern under centralized management of a school system than under decentralization, where the customers (parents and students) are directly involved. When the money and the power is at the central office, parents must deal with a bureaucracy to transact business. But, when the money and the power are based at the school, parents deal directly with those who can make a difference. When each local school is under the watchful eye of the customers, there is greater hope that all energies and resources will be focused on educational, not bureaucratic, needs. As a matter of fact, the continuing presence of parents on local school advisory committees provides a buffer against reckless union power thrusts, and presents another voice in support of students.

The educational constituency is enlarged

Although during the early stages of decentralization school communities tend to act in a parochial manner and focus only on their own school needs and not the needs of the larger system, this shortsighted view is not permanent. Sooner or later, all of the local school committees will discover that they share an overriding common interest—better education. The next logical step is to organize on a system-wide basis to lobby for increased support for the schools and increased freedom for parents to have a choice in their children's education.

The superintendent can speed this process by organizing an advisory committee that meets with him on a regular basis. The committee can be structured in two tiers. The first tier is a large group composed of delegates from every local school advisory committee. This group meets periodically to deal with issues of system-wide scope and to receive needed information regarding the whole school system. The second group is a smaller one composed of members from the larger group. This smaller group meets regularly with the superintendent.

Through this arrangement, several developments take place. First, the superintendent receives feedback vital to the welfare of the system. Second, the advisory committees receive information vital to the local schools. Third, the two bodies spur creation of a lobby group of political activists for better education.

School based management means "effective schools"

Researchers have identified over 200 schools which meet the definition of an "effective school." To be an effective school, according to this research, the percentage of students from low-income backgrounds who learn essential skills needed to succeed in the next grade level must be close to the percentage of students from middle and upper-income backgrounds who are mastering the same essential skills.

The Effective School Movement began about 15 years ago when a number of reputable educators wanted to prove that schools do make a difference. They began to look for schools in which equal proportions of low-income students and middle-to-upper income students were achieving mastery of the essential (basic) skills. The educators were able to identify a number of these schools. At that point the researchers tried to determine what there was about an "effective" school that was different from an "ineffective" school. To this day, educators are continuing to identify and study effective schools. Educators continue to identify, to study, and to try to develop effective schools.

The Effective Schools research has concluded that effective schools have the following five broad characteristics:

- Strong instructional leadership
- High expectations
- Instructional focus
- Positive school climate
- Measurement of effectiveness

These five characteristics are referred to as the "correlates" of an effective school, because these characteristics have a relationship (correlation) to an effective school. Although researchers cannot prove that these characteristics *cause* a school to be effective, they can prove that these correlates are present in the schools found to be "effective".

A successful school based management program promotes all of these correlates. School based management encourages a principal to become a more effective instructional leader by becoming more entrepreneurial and creative, and by using effective tactics of collaboration. Joint "ownership" of the school by parents, students, faculty, and principal tends to raise expectations. School based management is based upon goals related to student learning. As a result, local school plans do have a definite instructional focus. Because school based management is based upon collaboration among stakeholders, a democratic school climate arises in which team cooperation increases. Finally, no school based management program is complete without a comprehensive evaluation program which measures specific results in the individual schools. School based management is an excellent means for achieving "effective schools."

Does School Based Management Make a Difference in Student Learning?

This is the important question asked most often by those who keep the purpose of education firmly in view. In the chapter on the evaluation of school based management, "customer evaluation" is discussed as the bottom line evaluation. If all the main partners and stakeholders in the schools (students, parents, teachers, administrators, and board members) all *believe* that decentralized management is better than centralized management, then chances are that they are right. American culture considers customer satisfaction, in most instances, to be the final proof of success.

However, that's not good enough for some people who want "scientific" *proof* that school based management causes better student learning. These people demand a valid statistical study which proves that there is a causal relationship between decentralized management and improved student learning.

On the surface, such a demand sounds reasonable. After all, just pleasing everybody is not enough. Unfortunately, at this time there is no clear empirical evidence which proves that school based management enhances student learning, and it is likely to be a long time before researchers find that evidence. First of all, the transition to school based management is a drawn-out process. Secondly, the factors which affect student learning are quite complex. Health, family environment, economic status, intelligence, changing school programs, etc., all affect student learning. It will be difficult to isolate one factor, the complex issue of school based management, and prove that it enhances student learning.

However, there is some evidence which indicates that school based management does improve student learning. School based management requires the meaningful involvement of parents in the affairs of the schools. Now, there are many reasons to work closely with parents under school based management, but the most important reason is that *parent involvement has a powerful effect on student achievement.** Not only do children whose parents are involved do better throughout their entire school careers, but schools that work well with families have lower drop-out rates and higher test scores. In 1981, the National Committee for Citizens in Education (NCCE) published *The Evidence Grows,* an annotated bibliography describing 35 studies on the subject. The findings were all positive—parent involvement in almost any form improves student achievement.

In 1987, NCCE did an update, *The Evidence Continues to Grow: Parent Involvement Improves Student Achievement.* It includes 49 studies that, taken together, place the conclusion beyond dispute. Programs that include strong parent involvement produce students who perform better than otherwise identical programs that do not involve parents. Schools that relate well to their communities have student bodies that outperform other schools. Children whose parents help them at home and stay in touch with the school score higher than children of similar apti-

---

* *Workbook on Parent Involvement for District Leaders,* by Anne T. Henderson and Carl L. Marburger, The National Committee for Citizens in Education, 1991, p. 7.

tude and family background whose parents are *not* involved. Schools where children are failing, improve dramatically when parents are called in to help. The main benefits, then, of parent involvement are:

- Higher grades and test scores
- Long-term academic improvement
- Positive attitudes and behavior
- More successful programs, and
- More effective schools

There Are a Number of Disadvantages to School Based Management

As has been stated in this book several times, no school district should embark upon school based management unless there is general agreement that change is needed and that decentralization is the way to go. There are many fine school districts in America which are doing as well as should be expected and there is little reason for major change in their way of doing things. Naturally, there is always room to improve, but a drastic change in the management system may not be needed, especially considering the effort that such a change requires and the potential risk that the system may not improve or may get worse.

The restructuring of a school district's management system through decentralization is a serious decision and should involve all parties associated with the enterprise. The potential for conflict, misunderstanding, and political mischief is considerable, if the educational family is not bound by a strong sense of trust and credibility. Before entering into school based management, a number of considerations should be examined.

Preparation requires significant planning time and effort

The usual approach is organizing a task force to study various approaches to management restructuring before making a decision. Such task forces require that its members invest many hours of work. This extra time will be taken either from the members' professional or private schedules. In any case, these people should not be asked to contribute time and effort unless their recommendations will be given serious consideration. Improperly done, the mammoth effort of the task force could be wasted. This can produce more harm, in the form of disappointment and bitterness, than if the matter had never been initiated.

Extra financial assistance is needed to finalize a recommendation

To do the job right, a task force needs some funding. Members need to visit school districts that have been successful and unsuccessful in school based management. Research materials need to be purchased for study. If the task force meets during school hours, money must be available to pay substitutes for task force members who are teachers. Furthermore, no task force should try to make recommendations without the help of a successful, recognized school based management consultant. Without a consultant, the district will make the same mistakes that others have made. Although the cost of retaining such professional support should be small, the small investment can produce great returns.

Extra time on the part of everybody is required initially

Teachers and parents must serve on site committees. Principals must not only serve on such committees, but must learn how to write school plans, develop school budgets, follow new bookkeeping procedures, and learn new skills of leadership through collaboration. Some central office personnel will need extra time to shift from a "directing" to a "consulting" mode and will feel some frustration. If all of this effort eventually results in a return to business as usual, a great deal of skepticism and frustration will arise.

An inevitable increase in the workload of personnel during the initial stages of school based management, but a return to a more normal level can be expected after a successful transition. Some may ask, "Doesn't school based management increase the workload of principals and won't this increase take away from the principal's role as 'educational leader'?" The answer is "yes" and "no". Yes, the principal will work harder and longer during the transition period, but no, the principal will not have a heavier workload after school based management has been mastered. As a matter of fact, principals generally should find their jobs more satisfying.

Interviewing of a group of principals in the Edmonton, Alberta (Canada) Public Schools on this issue revealed some valuable information. (The reader will recall that Edmonton is an excellent model of school based management.) The principals interviewed had been principals under the previous administration which was centralized and remained principals under a new decentralized system. Not a single principal interviewed wanted to go back to the previous system. The principals reported that they didn't work "harder" under school based management, but they did work "smarter". One principal said he worked longer hours as a result of school based management, but that he did so because he wanted to, because he now felt an "ownership" of the school. He explained that under the previous system, he worked overtime because of his boss's demands for pointless activities, but that now he worked overtime because his efforts actually resulted in a better school.

The transition will probably involve controversy

When change is being contemplated, there is often an initial reactionary "knee-jerk" question: "What's in it for *me*?" When faced with change, many want to know if they will be "winners" or "losers". This self-serving, but understandable and realistic, response can be a serious threat to needed change. The "winners" will push for change and the "losers" will resist change. With patience, skill, and negotiations, this conflict will pass, especially if the superintendent sets a proper tone and exercises real leadership. However, the school board should be warned that a period of controversy is inevitable and that the board should not overreact to every accusation it hears.

Labor relations may become a problem

Sooner or later, school based management and collective bargaining rights will conflict. What is in the best interest of school based management might not be in the best interest of collective bargaining, and vice versa. For example, a site committee might agree in theory that more teacher supervision of students in the cafeteria is needed. However, the labor contract may have a provision which not only assures teachers of a duty-free lunch period, but may also prohibit teachers from providing such "sub-professional" services. Or, the union might propose during contract negotiations that no teacher be allowed to serve on a site committee which meets after regular working hours. Obviously, such a proposal would limit the flexibility of local site committees.

Should many such conflicts arise between school based management and collective bargaining rights, the tension could undermine seriously the success of decentralization. Therefore, there should be a prior agreement between management and union regarding how to limit such conflicts and how to resolve those that do arise. Again, it's the superintendent's job to explain all of this to the school board, and to encourage the school board not to overreact to hostile rumors it may hear from either side of the bargaining table.

Organizational inefficiency can result

School districts which are highly centralized in their management organization and led by an autocratic superintendent can appear to be very efficient, since the superintendent does not tolerate the "inefficiencies" of more democratic approaches. Everybody goes by the rule book or follows orders, no matter if rule book or the boss is wrong. This management style does get things done—and often gets them done quickly!

When management is decentralized and democratized, it looks as if "everybody gets into the act." This can cause decision making delays, inefficient day-to-day operations, and conflicts where none appeared to exist before. For example, in a centralized purchasing system where instructional supplies are purchased centrally based upon some formula which gives each school its fair share, purchasing generally operates efficiently. However, when individual schools have their own budgets for supplies, each school may request something different, thus making the handling of orders a new and additional burden on the central office. This may seem inefficient, but the apparent inefficiency needs to be weighed against another value—the value of allowing each school to purchase supplies which it needs, rather than supplies which the central office *believes* that the school needs.

There is no guarantee that things will be better

Successful decentralization may not improve overall school system operations significantly. Although improvements are likely school based management does not guarantee that staff morale will be better, that student test scores will improve, that teachers will perform better, that innovative programs will emerge, or that the tax dollar will be used more productively.

Yes, there are risks and potential disadvantages to school based management, just as there are in making other changes in the status quo. Any school district sincerely interested in the decentralization of its management system should weigh the possible gains against the possible losses. However, if done properly, there is little chance that the overall quality of the school district will decline because of school based management.

School Based Management Can Fail

Converting a school system from a highly centralized form of administration to a highly decentralized form is a drastic change in the way the organization operates. The change can be a threat to each special interest group within the system, opening the door to serious resistance and a risk of failure.

The following are the potential hazards which pose the greatest threats in attempting to convert to school based management:

Failure of the school board to support the management system

If the board does not support school based management, the program is doomed. A board might have trouble with the decentralization of management for any of a number of reasons. First, the board may not understand what it has gotten itself into. This often happens because the board does not take sufficient time to really grasp the implications of a changed management system. This is why an orientation program for the board is so important. Second, school based management, if not carried out properly, can bring special problems to the board, so some board members might begin to question the value of the new management system. Third, the board may be so deeply involved in the daily administration of the schools, that "letting go" is a practical impossibility. Fourth, since school based management results in diversity among the schools, the board may face serious dilemmas surrounding the issue of educational *equity*. In other words, if each school is allowed to be different, what assurance is there that each child has his or her fair (equitable) share of the educational pie?

The fourth point made here is very important. The main concern among board members considering decentralized management is how to assure educational fairness under a school based system. Under a centralized system, in which schools tend to be similar, being a board member is easier, because practically any action of the board applies to all schools. For example, if Algebra I is grouped in one school, it will be grouped in all schools. Everybody in the system is treated the same. However, under school based management, one school, after a proper collaborative process at the school level, might want to group Algebra I, while another school might believe that it has good reason not to group Algebra I. This "problem" is made even more pronounced when there is a high rate of student transfer from school to school within the school system.

Planners can deal with this problem by setting reasonable parameters in advance on what matters are centrally decided and what matters are left to the discretion of the local school. As one example of many, a school board might decide, before implementing school based management, that the food service (lunch) program will continue to be administered centrally. Or, a board might decide that student transportation will continue to be a central office function. However, that same board might agree in advance that all purchase of instructional supplies consumed in the schools will be left to the general discretion of the local schools, as long as such purchases are legal and within applicable regulations.

The superintendent's inability or unwillingness to "let go"

There are over 15,000 school superintendents in the American public school system. Obviously not all of these men and women will function the same way or see eye-to-eye on every educational issue. Some superintendents don't understand school based management, and some who do understand it, don't want anything to do with. The conventional view of an effective superintendent is one who is strong, decisive, and *makes things happen*. Many think a good superintendent is one who knows how to use power and make people do things with which they don't necessarily agree. Most school boards, when hiring a new superintendent, make it clear that they don't want a wimp. They want a chief executive officer who will run the school system (within the tolerance of the board) and "make things happen".

Given these views, is it any wonder that many superintendents are people who may resist school based management which they see as a threat to their power and authority? Is it any wonder that a career superintendent is reluctant to change his or her ingrained style of management? In an autocratic system, a "strong" and "decisive" superintendent may be what is needed, but in a democratic and decentralized system, a different set of skills are needed. And, too, what many superintendents fail to understand is that when "letting go" is done right, the superintendent not only becomes more effective but also becomes more powerful. In the context of school based management, "letting go" is a process of synergism, which means that the simultaneous action of separate forces together has greater total effect than the sum of the individual effects. In simpler terms, it means that a superintendent can get more good out of the system by effective delegation and sharing than by autocratic control.

The absence of an appropriate organizational structure

Throughout this book there are suggestions on how to reorganize for decentralized management. School based management requires redrawing the organizational chart of the school system, rewriting job descriptions, restructuring the financial accounting system, and changing program evaluation. If these changes are not made to accommodate school based management, the success of the program is threatened.

Unworkable and unfair allocation of resources to the schools

If money is not allocated to the schools fairly, school based management cannot work. Therefore, to reduce this risk, the superintendent should place this matter at the top of the priority list, and school based management should not be attempted until the superintendent, central office administrators, principals, and teachers (and parents to a lesser degree) work together to develop an allocation system which they all view as fair. The superintendent should then present and explain the system to the board and encourage members' comments and advice.

Poor labor relations

Productive site management, especially when decentralized, requires harmonious relationships between teachers and the principal, and between the union and the central office. Local management thrives on trust and respect and withers with suspicion and animosity. If there is an adversary relationship in the school, the conflict will use up efforts better spent on improving the quality of education. In this climate, unions suspect management of looking for ways of circumventing the labor contract, and management thinks the union is putting its own welfare above that of the students. Therefore, when considering management decentralization, the board and superintendent should assess the quality of relations between teachers and principals, and between the union and management. In any case, however, both parties must observe the existing labor contract (unless there is agreement to do otherwise) and any applicable collective bargaining law.

Inadequate provision of staff development

Thorough staff development is vital to successful school based management. The board, the superintendent, the management staff, teachers (and other employees), parents, and students (generally, secondary students) need to be prepared for and trained in the skills needed for collaborative management.

Customer satisfaction is the acid test of any management system

If the customers are satisfied, the school district can carry on its business with little resistance. However, if the school community is unhappy with the schools, the schools must apply their efforts in putting out fires. The superintendent must design a system which measures precisely the level of satisfaction with the schools and must work to raise that level each year. Since each school community has a different population, school based management offers better hope for customer satisfaction than does a centralized system.

Lack of preparation

The greatest threat to the spread of decentralized management is the likelihood that many school districts will jump on the school based management bandwagon with limited knowledge and preparation. In such instances, the chance of failure is great, and each such failure will be viewed as proof that school based management does not work. Any management approach which puts an organization "out of control" is poor management and cannot continue. If the simple guidance provided in this book is followed, the chances of losing control are remote.

Chapter 5

Requirements for Success

Chapter Three presented a comprehensive definition of school based management, listing and discussing some thirteen elements of school based management. But for school based management to succeed, certain major organizational elements must be in place. These elements have been determined through the experiences of converting a large school district from a highly centralized form of administration to a highly decentralized one, and of working with school systems which have succeeded at school based management and are as follows:

- Effective operation within a decentralized management structure
- A clear purpose understood and supported by the school system and its communities
- An effective process for identifying and adopting goals aimed at better education
- An effective decentralized management structure
- A clear, published, and understood description of authorities and responsibilities
- Effective program planning
- Effective collection and utilization of information
- Effective resource allocation procedures
- A useful financial accounting system
- Practical staff development

- Productive labor relations
- An effective monitoring program
- An evaluation program based on results—not methodology
- Sound principles of organization
- A high degree of satisfaction among parents, students, and staff

Let's examine each of these elements.

Effective Operation within a Decentralized Management Structure

School based management does not require any substantive changes the in way a school board operates. The board continues to adopt policies and approve budgets, to hire and fire the superintendent and all other employees, to review disputes which come before it, and to oversee the school system's activities generally. In other words, the local school board remains in charge of the local school system, notwithstanding management decentralization.

Since school based management is basically an *executive* function, it is not a matter with which the board should become directly and routinely involved. Having said this, however, there are certain modifications which a board needs to make to support school based management while also protecting its own legitimate powers and responsibilities. Some of those actions called for under school based management are:

- The board should authorize a feasibility/advisability study before any change is made in the management system.
- The board should adopt a policy approving school based management in general terms and clear parameters, once school based management has been sanctioned.
- The board should involve itself in a learning program about school based management. No school board should authorize any drastic change in a management system unless it understands what it is doing.

- The board should set broad goals for the school system, which give the locals schools needed direction.

- The board should be prepared to entertain requests to adopt, modify, waive, or rescind policies which support school based management and are in the best interests of the system.

- The board should review all annual school plans and accompanying annual school budgets. Although the entire school system budget needs to be officially approved by the board, school plans need not be approved by the board. These plans, however, should be at least reviewed by the board and any opinions about those plans should be discussed with the superintendent. The board should be aware, however, that if it officially and specifically approves each annual school plan, it inserts itself into the day-to-day operation of each school. Also, by approving these plans, the board is taking on a share of the responsibility for the success or failure of those plans.

- The board should require regular and appropriate reports from the superintendent regarding the progress of school based management in order to retain oversight.

Clear Purpose Understood and Supported by the School and Community

Research has found that one of the characteristics of effective schools is the presence of a clear purpose. In these schools, staff members, students, and parents are committed to the same purpose. This clarity of purpose is the result of collaboration and can be published in the form of a "mission statement", which clearly states the intentions of the schools and which is supported by all parties. This mission statement sets a direction for the school system and serves as a guide for adopting specific goals.

Effective Process for Identifying and Adopting Goals Aimed at Better Education

Under decentralized management, goals for the school system come from many sources. The school board has an obligation to set broad goals for which all schools and departments should strive. The improvement of reading ability for students might be one example of a school board goal. The superintendent may have goals, too. An example of such a goal might be to streamline the evaluation process for management personnel. Individual departments in the central office might also have their own goals. One example for a finance department might be to establish a new auditing system. Each school should have its own unique goals. For example, a school might set as one of its goals to improve student behavior in the cafeteria.

It is the responsibility of the superintendent to establish an efficient process which allows all of these goals to be finalized at the appropriate times.

Effective Decentralized Management Structure

The organizational chart of a decentralized school system should be "flat"; that is, it should have as few layers as administratively advisable between the school principal and the superintendent. The structure should be responsive to the internal and external needs of the organization. Design of the chart should be the task of the superintendent alone.

Clear, Published, and Understood Description of Authorities and Responsibilities

When position descriptions are written, they should be based on the principle that *reform and creativity are more likely to occur when carried out by responsible, accountable parties*. It is understandable that principals, for example, can be expected to have little concern for programs and requirements for which they have no interest or accountability. And, when decisions are in the process of being made, *those affected by decisions should have a voice in those decisions*. For example, if the reading program is thought to need revision, teachers should be the most important group consulted before a final decision is made.

Effective Program Planning

Once the school system sets its goals, procedures must be in place for achieving those goals. How this is done will vary from school system to school system. For example, in large school districts there may be a special office in the central bureaucracy for program planning. In other districts, program planning may be spread among several units.

Effective Collection and Utilization of Information

Now that computers are well entrenched in most school districts, there is little excuse for lacking ready access to needed information. Not only can a school system generate its own internal information, it can also obtain, for little cost, valuable information from outside commercial sources. *There is a direct link between the quality of a decision and the amount and quality of relevant information available and used in making the decision.* Ideally, under decentralized management, each school should have its own ample computer equipment and should be tied in with a central "mainframe" to obtain legitimate and needed information. Large systems may have their own data centers, while small districts might need to pool their efforts for certain purposes.

Effective Resource Allocation Procedures

There are several ways to accomplish this, and one recommended way is described in Chapter Ten of this book. Whatever procedure is used, school districts should keep this in mind: *There is a direct correlation between the amount of money allocated to the schools and the school system's commitment to school based management.* If the local schools do not have sizeable allocations from which to build their own budgets, there is a serious doubt about the belief that school system has in real decentralized management. Serious management decentralization is not possible without *setting aside the largest share of the school system budget to the schools.*

Useful Financial Accounting System

Most school districts today have "program based" budgets, rather than "school based" budgets. This means that the school system budget is allocated to "programs" such as special education, language arts, personnel, maintenance, student transportation, construction, supply services, adult education, pupil personnel, safety and security, etc. Under this arrangement, the central office holds the major powers, and it is difficult to determine just how much is being spent on each school. Under "school based" budgeting, the largest portion of the entire school system's operation budget is allocated to the individual schools. This not only transfers power to the schools, but it comes closer to showing how much money is actually being spent in each school. This approach to budgeting, if carried out on a "student based" allocation, also assures greater student equity in the distribution of funds.

A conversion from program budgeting to school based budgeting requires major changes in the financial accounting system. Unless these changes are made properly, the success of school based management can be undermined. Even though the process of "student based" allocations is discussed elsewhere in Chapter Ten, no school district should attempt such a conversion without thorough preparation and training for all of those affected by the new financial accounting system.

Practical Staff Development

Several critical areas in moving to decentralized management hold the potential for failure. One real threat to school based management is insufficient training for the board, the superintendent, the central staff, faculties, principals, students, and parents. The board needs to understand how decision making shifts to the schools. Superintendents need to learn how to "let go." Central office personnel need to learn how to become consultants rather than directors. Principals need to learn how to lead through collaboration and how to prepare a school plan and budget. Teachers, students, and parents need help in carrying out their increased role in school management.

Generally speaking, staff development for school based management consists of orientation, strategic planning, financial planning, management/leadership skills, group and collaborative planning, purchasing, personnel management, and effective school training. More details on staff development are provided elsewhere in this book.

Productive Labor Relations

The success or failure of school based management will be played out on the labor relations field, primarily with teacher unions. The key question will be how much collective bargaining will interfere with the new non-adversarial and collaborative relationship that decentralized management requires. If teacher unions become hostile toward school based management, the potential for mischief and lost opportunity is great. Having said this, however, the fact is that collective bargaining is a legal requirement in forty-one states (and it exists to some degree in all other states), and these legal requirements must be obeyed.

Effective Monitoring Program

Unless a good monitoring program is in place, school based management can result in chaos, with each school doing what it wants and the central office not knowing what each school is doing. As is true in any organization, the boss must know what is going on and must have the power to make things happen when necessary. Under school based management, principals are responsible to a supervisor to whom they must submit reports. Detailed records are needed to show how the schools are spending their money. The central office needs to know that all legal requirements (e.g., special education) are being met. Attendance records are still needed. Student information files must be maintained, and so on and so forth. As a matter of fact, the monitoring function under school based management is fundamentally as comprehensive as under a more centralized system, but it requires a different approach.

Under decentralized management, program budgets still exist in the central office (although they are reduced), but one budget is added for each school in the school system. Along with the transfer of funds to the schools go increased decision making powers, so the central office must establish means for monitoring the activities of those schools. True, even in a centralized system of management, the superintendent needs to know what is happening in the schools, but under decentralization the potential for diversity is greatly increased, making monitoring in some ways more difficult.

One of the greatest threats to school based management is a failure to monitor and to intervene when needed. One of the sure ways that a superintendent can get into serious trouble with the school board is to lose touch with what is happening in the schools. When this happens, events bypass the superintendent and go directly to the board. This can be the beginning of a breakdown in the executive function of the school system.

Evaluation Program Based on Results—Not Methodology

Before a board agrees to school based management, it should require, among other things, to see just how the success of the new system will be measured.

The best way to judge the success of school based management is:

- to survey students, parents, and employees annually concerning their views about their schools, and

- to examine indicators (e.g., standardized tests) of student learning annually.

A fuller explanation of how to evaluate school based management is found in Chapter Twelve.

Sound Principles of Organization*

For school based management to work well, it must operate according to certain sound principles of organization. When these principles are published, understood, and subscribed to, they provide an efficient framework within which actions are taken.

A. Generally, multiple criteria, which are frequently conflicting, are to be considered when making and carrying out decisions. The major criteria to be considered when making and carrying out decisions are the mission statements of the district.

B. Every individual in the organization shall know the results for which that person is responsible. Both objectives and evaluations should be focused upon those results.

C. Each individual in the organization shall have only one supervisor.

An individual can seek advice, guidance, and assistance from anyone, but no one other than that person's direct line supervisor shall have the authority to set objectives, allocate resources, direct or veto decisions or actions, and evaluate that person's performance.

D. Communications should be kept as free and open as possible. Any person in any part and at any level of the organization should be encouraged to communicate to any other person or part of the organization for information or assistance needed to perform that person's job. "Going through channels" is not applicable to these situations, provided the immediate supervisor is informed as appropriate.

E. Authority can be delegated. The delegation of authority does not in any way diminish the responsibility the delegator had prior to the delegation. Individuals with similar positions need not have similar degrees of authority. Delegation of

---

*These principles of organization are a published statement of the Edmonton, Alberta (Canada) Public Schools and are reprinted with permission.

authority can be individualized to match differing levels of performance.

F. No one shall have the authority to direct or veto any decision or action where that person is not responsible for the results.

G. The organization should avoid uniform rules, practices, policies, and regulations which are designed to protect the organization against "mistakes". Such provisions tend to be designed with the least competent individuals in mind, and their uniform application will tend to force all individuals to perform uniformly at the lowest common level.

H. Each member of the leadership team shall promote and maintain a strong relationship of mutual trust, confidence, and respect among all members of the organization. Each member of the leadership team shall actively pursue the foregoing with respect to all staff members under that person's supervision.

I. Every individual in the organization shall behave with absolute integrity in that person's relationship with all others—both within and outside the organization. An individual shall not knowingly or carelessly, by omission or commission, misinform or mislead, withhold information which should be disclosed, or do anything else to cause doubts upon the honesty, integrity or motives of the organization or any of its individual members.

High Degree of Satisfaction among Students, Parents, and Staff

In other words, the customers must be reasonably happy. One of the positive aspects of American life is the presence of private companies competing to see which one can satisfy the customer best. Without customer satisfaction, a private company eventually will go out of business. However, public schools cannot go out of business no matter how bad they may become. It is the only game in town. There are laws which keep public schools in business even when their customers are dissatisfied.

Therefore, to avoid such an unhappy situation, the public schools must first set a means by which to measure customer satisfaction, and then set about to increase that satisfaction. Even though the public school system is a *de facto* monopoly, it nevertheless has an obligation to service its diverse customer base. School based management offers greater hope to satisfy a diverse community than does a highly centralized administration. In the final analysis, if the customer is unhappy, the schools have failed.

Instructions on how to measure customer satisfaction, along with actual survey forms, are found in Chapter Twelve.

Chapter 6

Parameters

No school board should allow school based management to be adopted as its management structure without a clear understanding of that structure. Although school based management is an executive function, and therefore the board should not interfere, some special problems can arise if school based management is not structured properly and carried out correctly within clear limits or parameters.

It should be made clear at the beginning that definite limits will be placed on what schools can do in the name of school based management. However, these parameters should be few and broad.

- *All school plans must be legal.* This is not a new parameter, since all laws must be obeyed regardless of the management structure.

- *All state regulations must be obeyed.* Only if there is permission from the state should a school system do otherwise. If a local school wishes to initiate a project which runs counter to some state regulation, it should request the local superintendent to ask the state for a waiver. Evidence from throughout the Unites States shows that such waivers are often granted in the name of sound educational innovation.

- *School accreditation requirements must be met.* However, existing accreditation requirements often allow for some deviation, and waivers can be sought.

- *School board policy must be obeyed.* This is true unless the board gives prior permission to do otherwise. But such permission is nothing new to school boards, which are often asked to modify, waive, or rescind a policy. Over a period of time, however, school based management, if successful, will likely put some additional pressure on the board to modify some of its policies to accommodate sound educational innovation.

- *Administrative regulations must be followed.* Only the superintendent can allow deviation. A superintendent who supports school based management should be open to any reasonable request to stray from a regulation in the interest of achieving a sound local school objective. Naturally, a superintendent cannot allow a school to deviate from a regulation if the action runs counter to a school board policy.

- *All contracts must be honored.* Unless all parties agree otherwise, all contracts, including the labor contract with employee unions, must be carried out. Many contracts, including labor contracts, often include provisions for amendment.

- *Other appropriate parameters which the board and superintendent feel strongly about should be determined.* However, these parameters should be few in number. Since it has already been established that schools will follow all policies, regulations, and established administrative procedures unless otherwise approved, it is not necessary or advisable to make a long list of things which schools *cannot* do.

The development of an excessively long list of parameters is inadvisable for several reasons. First, the list could be endless, since the administration of a school system involves thousands of individual actions too numerous to list. Second, no finite list could be made, since a great deal of administrative trivia would be overlooked. Third, the making of such a list would be counterproductive to the encouragement of schools to be creative and different in response to the needs of their communities.

Having said this, however, if the board and superintendent are convinced that certain existing policies and practices should not be changed under any conditions, then those non-negotiable issues should be listed. For example, most school districts would not even consider a proposal from a school to operate its own student transportation system. Also, many school systems feel strongly that the food service (lunch) program should be managed centrally. Additionally, most school districts would be opposed to allowing individual schools to finance and manage capital maintenance and repair, such as roof replacement. Many schools systems would be hesitant to school base the payment of utilities. Or, as a final example, a school system might, for good reason, put the revision of student report cards beyond the discretion of the individual school.

There is nothing wrong with stating such obvious restrictions on school based management at the outset, avoiding unnecessary proposals and automatic rejections. However, once these obvious limits are published, everything else should be fair game to *propose*. In other words, anything not covered by the stated parameters can be placed in the school plan for the super-intendent's consideration. This approach does not open the barn door to reckless proposals; schools often are too timid in proposing changes! Once in a while, a ridiculous proposal may come in, but so what? It can easily be rejected, while leaving the door open to many good possibilities for change.

In other words, *a school can do anything that is in the approved school plan; otherwise, it's business as usual*. A school may propose any action, unless it is specifically prohibited by the published parameters, and any such proposal is entitled to serious discussion and consideration. If the proposal is approved, it becomes a part of the approved school plan. If the proposal is rejected, the school continues with "business as usual", and the *status quo* prevails. By following this logical and orderly approach to dealing with proposals for change, all good ideas are encouraged and considered, and the school system does not lose control. Anything less than the parameters discussed in this paragraph subjects the board and its administration to the risk of responsibility for improper actions.

In addition to the basic parameters of law, state regulations, accreditation standards, school board policy, administrative regulations, and contracts, what principles should be considered in deciding which decisions should be made at the school level and which should be made by the central office?

First of all, it should be understood that the overriding purpose of the public school system is to provide students with the best learning experiences possible. This is why schools are built—to serve the educational needs of students. Since the students are *in* the schools, every activity of the school system should be focused on the school as the basic unit. This means that the greatest share of the operating budget of the school system should be transferred to the schools along with corresponding decision-making powers. For example, if the local school is the budget-holder for instructional supplies, then the local school should have wide discretion in deciding what instructional supplies are needed.

In the model being discussed in this book, over 75% of the school system's budget is allocated to the schools. With this amount of money, the local school is charged with:

- The hiring and deployment of all personnel assigned to the school (subject to final approval by the school board)
- The payment of certain extra-curricular supplements
- The payment of substitutes for one to three days of consecutive absence
- The payment for textbooks
- School based staff development
- Student field trips

- All new and replacement school furniture and instructional equipment
- Repair of non-standard equipment
- Incidental maintenance needs of the building
- Instructional and administrative supplies
- Media center materials

This list is a *sample* list and is not meant to be fixed. It will vary from school system to school system, depending upon the wishes of each and the amount of money allocated to the schools. It should be kept in mind, however, that *there is a direct correlation between the amount of money allocated to the schools and the school system's commitment to school based management.* In other words, the more money distributed to the schools, the more likelihood of real decentralization of management.

As long as we have public school systems and public school boards, there will be central offices—school based management notwithstanding. That means that even under an advanced form of school based management, the central office will continue to retain significant funds and decision-making powers (and rightly so).

What then are the legitimate functions of the central office under an advanced form of decentralization? Under school based management, the central office functions should consist of :

- Responsibility for activities which have significant, fluctuating, or highly unpredictable costs
- Responsibility for certain services needed by the schools.

These guidelines indicate that the purpose of the central office is to increase the quality of education in the schools. Now let's examine each of these guidelines to determine which responsibilities should remain with the central office.

Responsibility for Activities which have Significant, Fluctuating, or Highly Unpredictable Costs

The application of this principle *spreads the risk* of unanticipated high cost items. For example, in most instances the payment for the repair of school roofs would not be the responsibility of the individual school. Roof repair is usually unpredictable, costs can fluctuate greatly, and the cost of roof repair can be very expensive. If individual schools were responsible for the repair of their own roofs, a local school budget could be wiped out by the cost of replacing its roof. There would be little money left over to run the school. Therefore, roof repair and replacement should be the responsibility of the central office.

All repair and replacement of capital equipment should be the responsibility of the central office. This includes, but is not necessarily limited to, the repair and replacement of heating and air-conditioning systems, floors, windows, doors, parking lots, property fences, building structures, driveways, sidewalks, rest room equipment, cafeteria equipment, and other fixed capital equipment above a certain cost. As all of these items can be costly to repair or replace and often break down without warning, the local school should be relieved of the risks which come with the responsibility for these items. By centralizing these responsibilities, the risks (that is, the unanticipated costs) can be spread among all the schools. In that way, all schools are treated equitably. All schools get replacements and repairs as needed, and no school faces expensive surprises.

While the central office should be responsible for the repair and replacement of fixed capital equipment *above a specified cost*, each school should be given an allotment for the repair of non-fixed equipment *below* a specified cost. For example, it is logical under school based management to have the school bear the cost of repairing certain non-fixed equipment, like instructional equipment (overhead projectors, VCR's, etc.). This does not mean necessarily that the school has such items repaired by private vendors. All this equipment can be repaired through the central office, but the cost is charged to the school. Experience with school based management indicates that most purchases made by the individual school are from the school system's own repair and supply services.

In addition to the responsibilities already mentioned, the central office should also assume the responsibility for general school liability, property insurance, Workers' Compensation, emergency expenditures (reserve fund), and the salary reserve fund.

Responsibility for Certain Services Needed by the School

Even under school management which has been decentralized, the individual schools need certain services which logically should be provided by the central office. For example, under school based management, each school has its own budget. Although each school records its own spending, this record is not correct until purchases have been made and charged against the school. The central office keeps a record of all spending by individual schools, and must give each school a monthly school budget status report. Otherwise, the school would be uncertain whether it was staying within its approved budget. That's one example of a responsibility the central office should assume under the premise that the schools need certain assistance which can be provided best by the central office.

There are many services which the central office should provide for the schools. The following list is meant to serve only as a sample.

- Preparation, publication, and distribution of school board policies and regulations
- Certification of substitute teachers
- Initial screening of all employment candidates
- New teacher orientation
- Employee recruitment

- Employee payroll
- Employee fringe benefit program
- School system budget development
- Regular budget reports
- School audit reports
- Information reports from data processing
- School population data
- Public relations assistance
- Worker safety programs
- Property security
- Planning, design, and construction of capital improvements
- Employee fringe benefits administration
- Centralized purchasing
- Supply warehousing
- Student transportation
- Plant maintenance (above a specified cost)
- Food service program
- Inter-school courier service
- Repair of standard (approved) equipment
- System-wide curriculum development and supervision
- Non-school based alternative education
- Non-school based summer school
- Standard student testing program
- Non-school based staff development
- Negotiations, contract supervision, and grievances
- Adult education

- Specified pupil personnel services (psychological services, student transfer appeals, etc.)
- Specified special education services (due process appeals, VI-B Funds, occupational and physical therapy, and other itinerant services)
- Instructional technology support
- Chapter I funds
- Responsibilities for obligations placed on the central office from outside the school system (for example, completion of state and federal reports)
- Other appropriate responsibilities which help the schools provide better education

In summary, the process of deciding where to assign responsibilities under decentralized management is a difficult task. Where a given responsibility should be placed is not always a clear issue. For example, in a given school system, the curriculum could be a parameter. In other words, the determination of curriculum is a central responsibility and the schools must observe a system-wide curriculum. Under this arrangement, where is the responsibility for textbooks? The school district might decide to assign the purchase of the textbooks to the local schools, or it might decide to administer the textbook program centrally. A case can be made for either.

There is an obvious advantage to allowing the schools to be the budget-holders for the purchase of textbooks. In this way, schools are much more careful in the number of books they order and in protecting books from loss and damage. If the textbooks are provided "free" from the central office, there is less such concern. However, even when the schools are the budget-holders for textbooks, the actual ordering of the books can be coordinated centrally to benefit from bulk purchases.

On the other hand, a case can be made for allowing the central office to be responsible for the textbook program. It's difficult to distribute funds to the schools on a "student based" allocation, since all of the schools vary somewhat in their textbook needs. Some schools may have books in reserve, some may have all new books, some may have old books, some may lose and damage books more than other schools, and some may distribute textbooks to students in different ways. Consequently, a school district might find it more logical to direct the textbook program from the central office.

As a school system enters into school based management, all of the people associated with developing the school plan and budget (teachers, parents, students, and principal) should know exactly what limits are imposed upon their discretion. These limits should be developed through collaboration so that the schools do not feel that they are being dictated to arbitrarily. Once these boundaries on school authority have been set, each school should be encouraged to propose innovative ways to respond to the educational needs of the community.

This approach will bring to the superintendent proposals which have never been considered before under a more centralized system of management where rules govern everything. Once the schools learn that they can actually propose their own ideas, the superintendent will be faced with a continuing and endless stream of proposals, each of which will have to be decided on its own merits. This can be a real dilemma for the superintendent, for on the one hand the superintendent will want to approve the requests of local schools, but on the other hand, the superintendent, as the chief executive officer, must be concerned with the larger issue of the whole school system. Furthermore, the superintendent must consider the views of the school board. But with diligence, a commitment to a belief in empowering the school, and good faith among all parties, the right decision usually will be made. And, in most cases, if the wrong decision is made, it can be corrected.

Chapter 7

Launching the Process

The question of how to convert to school based management is critical, but it is difficult to provide an answer which would fit over 15,000 different school systems ranging in size from those with only a few students to those with over 100,000. Some of these school systems are highly centralized, while others are not.

Despite the wide diversity among school systems, however, it is possible to make certain general suggestions which should help in most situations.

Propose Consideration of School Based Management

Someone or some group will come forward with a suggestion or request to consider an organizational restructuring. The request may mention school based management by name, or it may be referred to in some other way. The topic might be initiated by the school board, which could ask the superintendent to investigate the idea. Frankly, however, management decentralization is something school boards don't generally bring up for two reasons. First, management is a function of the superintendent's office; and second, many board members view school based management as an unneeded intrusion into the powers of the board.

The subject could be broached by the superintendent, who may be seeking ways to improve education through a restructured management system. Superintendents who are so inclined must be careful, however, not to use their authority to bring about restructuring unilaterally. A superintendent could order the establishment of school based management, but this autocratic approach would undermine the basic principles of school based management and therefore would not be likely to succeed. Rather, the superintendent should gather a representative group together, share views with the group, and then ask the members if they would be willing to look into the matter.

A group of teachers interested in school based management might recommend or request a study of the subject. If interest in the topic seems to be widespread, the superintendent may wish to sanction such a study officially and provide support. Naturally, the superintendent should inform the board of this development and seek a reaction.

Or, a request might come from the teachers' union either as a part of negotiations or separate from negotiations. Again, if there seems to be sufficient interest, a representative task force can be organized to investigate possibilities. It should be understood at the outset, however, that issues of management structure are not a mandatory topic of labor negotiations. School based management should *not* be developed in an adversarial atmosphere between only two parties, but ideally should come about with many parties working in a relationship of collaboration. In a growing number of cases, state legislatures are passing laws dealing with new management structures. Obviously, these laws must be followed. If state legislatures do intervene in local management issues, the laws should be very general, and should support the basic principles of decentralized and collaborative management. The more specific the state law gets, the more likely it is to conflict with a basic tenet of school based management: that those affected by a decision should have a voice in that decision.

Wherever the initiative comes from (unless directed by law), no school system should go forward unless there is strong evidence of significant interest in the restructuring.

Establish a Task Force

If there is a go-ahead to study the restructuring of management, a representative task force should be selected. The manner of selection is a matter for local decision. In any case, however, the task force must be generally representative of the central office staff, faculty and other staff, parents, students, and the professional and business community. A chairperson should be selected. Regardless of who it is, this person should have direct access to the superintendent to most effectively promote the important and official nature of the work the task force is undertaking.

Determine Guidelines for Task Force

The task force must get itself organized. This means it must:

- Determine its mission and objectives
- Set a deadline for completion of its recommendation
- Set up a calendar of meetings
- Decide what records will kept and how
- Make work assignments for each member
- Obtain from the superintendent resources needed for task force operations, such as visits to other school districts, seminar attendance, research materials, consultant fees, etc.

It is highly advisable to acquire the services of an experienced consultant to help the school system avoid the many mistakes that other school systems have made in their attempts to decentralize.

The budget for the task force doesn't need to be large. Funds should be available to visit school systems whose similar efforts have been successful. A small amount of money will be needed for purchasing and copying reading material, and some members should be encouraged to attend appropriate seminars. And, as stated earlier, a consultant should be available at critical points. Beyond that, the committee members, as intelligent and motivated people, should be able to fend for themselves.

Submit a Recommendation Report

The task force recommendation (which goes to the superintendent) should cover all aspects of why school based management is advisable, and how it will work. Some of the important areas which must be included in the report are:

- Should there be a pilot program? If so, why? If not, why not?
- The purpose of restructuring must be explained and defended.
- Parameters must be listed.
- New budgeting procedures need to be described.
- A new organizational chart should be drawn.
- Revised sample job descriptions should be included.
- A financial monitoring system should be described.
- A description of how funds will be allocated is a must.
- A monitoring procedure needs to be outlined.
- There must be an explanation of how the success of school based management will be measured.
- A staff development program must be included, incorporating the preparation of school plans and budgets, site committee training, new approaches to the principalship, new accounting procedures, etc.

The task force should present its complete report at a publicized, open hearing. In this way, everyone has the opportunity to present their views before the report is finalized. If the report does not have the unanimous support of the task force, those with dissenting or differing views should attach their rationale to the report.

Prepare a Final Report for School Board

When the report is ready, the superintendent should meet with the entire task force. This meeting gives members a chance to present and explain their recommendations and gives the superintendent an opportunity to ask questions. Assuming there is a recommendation to proceed with school based management, and assuming the superintendent agrees, the report should then be submitted to the school board. When the board receives the report it is advisable to have the task force present, so that members can help answer questions.

A superintendent who does not agree with the report has only three choices:

- Reject the report and terminate the task force and any study.
- Modify the report unilaterally, and take responsibility for what reactions that might cause.
- Attempt to persuade the task force to modify the report.

In any case, the superintendent must eventually report to the school board. Whether the superintendent has rejected, modified, or accepted the report of the task force, the board deserves an explanation.

The School Board Makes the Final Decision

Now it's up to the board. If the superintendent has recommended the report, an appropriate policy (or resolution) should be included for the board to adopt indicating its support of school based management. The following two policies are recommended.

SAMPLE MOTION TO STUDY SCHOOL BASED MANAGEMENT

Whereas there has been significant interest expressed by staff and parents regarding a method of school management often referred to as "school based management"; and

Whereas the Board is similarly interested in management plans which have the potential for educational improvement;

It is therefore moved that the Superintendent be authorized to organize a representative task force of staff, parents, students and community members to study the advisability of school based management. A complete report on this topic, including a description of school based management and a recommendation for action, accompanied by appropriate rationale, shall be submitted to the Board no later than June 1st.

SAMPLE SCHOOL BOARD POLICY REGARDING SCHOOL BASED MANAGEMENT

Based upon the report, "School Board Management," submitted to Board on June 1, 199__, the Board supports the management actions called for in that report, with the following requirements:

1. All Board policies shall be adhered to unless there is prior approval by the Board to do otherwise.

2. Any change from existing regulations will be reported to Board immediately by the Superintendent.

3. All "parameters" listed in the report, "School Based Management" (June 1, 199__) shall be adhered to unless there is prior approval of the Board to do otherwise.

4. All individual "school plans" as called for in the report shall be submitted to the Board for review prior to approval by the Superintendent.

5. By no later than June 1, 199__, the Superintendent shall submit to the Board a thorough report which evaluates the implementation of school based management.

Chapter 8

The School Site Committee

Under the model of school based management being discussed in this book, each school must have a "site" committee. The title of the committee can vary according to the wishes of the local school system. Such committees can be called "advisory committees," "school governance councils," "community forums," etc. Regardless of the title, however, the purpose of each such group is the same:

The purpose of the site committee is to create an "ownership" of the school by stakeholders. One of the main advantages of decentralized management is that those who have the most at stake in the school (that is, the parents, students, staff, and principal) have an opportunity to fashion the school according to the special needs of the community which the school serves. The value of this ownership is based upon two well-established principles:

- Innovation and reform are more likely when carried out by those who have ownership, responsibility, and accountability.

- Those affected by decisions should have a voice in making those decisions.

There is little doubt that schools are better with these site committees than without them. There is also little doubt that a school system managed by a highly centralized structure and autocratic methods does not bring out the best in students, parents, or staff. A public school system can be operated without serious input from its stakeholders, but in general, the school system will do better by taking advantage of the strength, knowledge, and good will of those who have a stake in the success of the schools.

All site committees share certain basic and required functions, which are:

The Committee Must Meet Regularly

The school community can decide how often the committee meets, but the committee must meet often enough to carry out its tasks.

The Committee Must Be Involved in the Preparation of the School Plan

Although people outside of the committee may give advice and energy, it is the committee's function to prepare the final school plan before submitting it to the superintendent.

The Committee Must Be Involved in Preparing the School Budget

It is important that the school plan and school budget go forward hand-in-hand. Otherwise, the two might not be compatible. Furthermore, if the committee does not involve itself in the school budget, there is always the chance that money could be budgeted without the knowledge of the committee.

The Committee Must Serve in an Advisory Capacity Regarding Other Important School Affairs

Each time the committee meets, the principal should provide a briefing on various aspects of the school program. Such reports will not only keep the committee informed, but will provide an opportunity for the panel to advise and assist the principal.

The Committee Composition Must Be Representative

Whether the institution is a high school or elementary school, a large school or a small school, the committee must include students, parents, staff, and the community at large. The school can decide how to pick the committee members, but members should be *representative*; that is, they should be in touch with the group from which they were chosen. For example, school staff members must serve on the committee, and they can be elected by the staff or chosen in some other manner acceptable to the committee.

Students are an important part of the committee. They, too, can be elected by the student body or chosen in another acceptable manner. For example, representatives might be appointed by the student government. There is no reason not to include students on site committees at the elementary level. Mature students at the 4th, 5th, and 6th grade levels can provide a valuable dimension to the group.

Parents, along with representatives of the community at large (business and professional), should serve on the committee. They, like all other members, should be selected in a way which assures balanced representation. In some cases, it will be necessary to "reach out" to some parents who may not come forward due to employment and family responsibilities, cultural orientation, or other factors which might make them reluctant to become involved in school affairs.

The principal should serve on the committee either as an official member or as an *ex-officio* member, but more is discussed about this topic later in this chapter.

Committees Can Be Different

For example, at a small elementary school, the committee could be one relatively small representative group which meets several times each year. However, at a large comprehensive high school, there might be several committees involving large groups of representatives. It should be made clear at this point, however, that as important as site committees are, they are not the only source of advice and help available to the school. For example, if the principal wants to call in a volunteer computer specialist for advice, the principal is free to do so. In any case, though, the site committee should be aware of and involved in those important decisions which affect the quality of education at the school.

The Committee's Powers Are Limited

The committee must stay within all laws, state regulations, school board policies, school system regulations, and contracts, including any labor contracts. Also, the committee must stay within the limits of the school budget. It cannot support spending money that the school does not have. Finally, the committee should be aware that its functions are carried out within the limits of authority of the school principal. For example, it would not do for the panel to require lower lunch prices, if lunch prices are set centrally. The committee must understand that actions not within the power of the principal must be discussed in another forum.

Certain Needs of the Committee Must Be Met

First, the committee must have the official sanction of the school system. This means that the local site committee has an official and important role in the management of the schools. Second, all committee members need training in how to function as a group. Third, the committee must have leadership from its chairperson. Fourth, the committee must have access to needed information. And fifth, the committee should have published ground rules (or bylaws).

Ground Rules Must Be Established

In order to focus the efforts of the committee, the group should agree to certain operational procedures, or bylaws. This document should answer at least the following questions:

- What is the purpose of the committee?
- What is the composition of the committee?

- How are members selected?
- What are the functions of the committee?
- How often shall the committee meet?
- How shall vacancies be filled?
- What officers are there and what are their duties?
- What is the role of *Robert's Rules of Order*, if any?
- How are the bylaws revised?

A sample of the bylaws of an elementary school committee are found at the end of this chapter.

The Chairperson's Role Must Be Clear

If the chairperson's role is *not* clear, members may waste effort on unproductive procedural and relationship matters. The chairperson's highest duty is to move the group toward its objective by using good leadership practices within the adopted bylaws and rules of good will. The chairperson should not dominate the meeting, but should show leadership by devising ways to get the best from each member of the group. The chairperson, with the help of the principal (if not the same person), should also be responsible for general matters such as keeping proper committee records, preparing agendas, notifying members, and doing anything else needed to make all meetings successful.

Choosing the Chairperson

Any member of the group can serve as chairperson, if that person has been selected by the group according to any applicable provisions in the bylaws. If the committee, with full knowledge of its action, chooses the school principal, that's O.K. But prior to making that decision, the committee should discuss openly whether the building principal necessarily is the best person to chair the committee. Under the type of school based management described in this book, it is recommended that the principal not serve as chairperson. The principal is the chief executive officer of the school, the one with the power to make decisions regarding the school, and the one held accountable for those decisions. A principal who also serves as chairperson of the advisory committee is in a position to control what advice he or she gets as principal. Also, by serving as chairperson of the committee, the principal runs the risk of blocking the best advice from the committee and of denying needed ownership of the committee by its members.

The suggestion that principals should not serve as chairpersons can be a sensitive issue for principals who view the suggestion as undermining the principal's legitimate authority. Such a concern is groundless. Everyone knows that the principal is responsible for the welfare of the school, that someone must be in charge, and that a principal cannot relinquish this accountability. A principal should not be threatened by allowing another committee member to serve as chairperson, any more than the committee members should be threatened because they must work within certain parameters. Regardless of who is chosen as chairperson, a sincere collaborative relationship between all members enhances the power of the principal and of the committee—and the students benefit.

An Appropriate Meeting Site Should Be Selected

Since the committee transacts official school business, the school should be the normal meeting place for the committee. By meeting at the school, technical support (copy machine, telephone, word processor, etc.) is available. This does not suggest, however, that the committee should never meet outside the school. There may be a number of special occasions when the committee may have good reason to meet elsewhere—for example, on the premises of a local business. Some committees have found it useful to hold meetings in the homes of members.

The Meeting Site Must Be Adequate

There must be table space to work on. Chairs should be reasonably comfortable. Temperature and lighting control should be adequate. Distractions in the form of noise, pedestrian traffic, etc., should be minimal. There should be access to rest rooms, and access to telephone for business calls and emergencies. A word processor or typewriter is often helpful in making drafts while the committee is in session. This, then, implies the need for a copy machine to duplicate materials for each member. A chalk board or butcher block paper and easel (with masking tape) are a must for productive group work. As far as refreshments are concerned, that's a matter for the group to consider.

Good Communication Is Essential

Agendas should be sent out in advance, minutes should be distributed, and there will be other documents to circulate among group members. Telephone numbers and addresses will need to be exchanged. A decision will need to be made as to how documents will be circulated. The U.S. Mail or the courier service of the school system can be used.

WESTRIDGE PLANNING COUNCIL BYLAWS*

Westridge Elementary School, Prince William County, VA

MISSION STATEMENT

The Westridge Planning Council is committed to working cooperatively toward fulfilling the Westridge Elementary School Philosophy.

BYLAWS FOR SCHOOL COUNCIL MEMBERS

Purpose

The bylaws will provide the Westridge Planning Council with an established set of rules/procedures under which to function.

---

*These bylaws are for demonstration only and are not necessarily appropriate for all schools.

Meetings

The Westridge Council shall meet the first Tuesday of each month in the school's conference room unless otherwise necessitated. Generally, the length of the meetings will be determined by the prepared agenda.

Agenda

A proposed agenda for the next meeting will be shared with the Council at the conclusion of each meeting. Members of the Council may suggest additional items to be added to the proposed agenda.

The chairperson or designee will prepare and distribute a copy to each member of the Council and one copy to the Division Planning Council at least two weeks prior to the next meeting.

Membership

Selection for community representation on the Council shall be by volunteers. In the event that there are more community representative volunteers than there are vacant seats, a lottery shall be held.

Team leaders and the media specialist will represent the staff on the council.

The membership on the Westridge Council shall include:

1. At least one parent representing each of the communities within the school boundaries.

2. The PTO Vice President in accordance with the bylaws of the PTO.

3. The principal, who will serve as the Chairperson of the Council.

4. One school staff person representing the classified personnel.

5. Eight team leaders representing the instructional staff.

Selection of Council Member Replacements

1. Parent/community representative: The Council shall seek volunteers for a vacant seat as prescribed under membership terms.
2. The parent/community representatives who volunteered to serve will be selected by lottery.
3. Staff representative: Positions for team leaders/Council representatives will be posted in the school, as terms expire or as positions become vacant prior to term expiration.
4. Effective Spring 1991, one half of the total representatives will be rotated beginning with team leaders of grades one, three, five, and community lottery.

Secretary

The position of secretary shall be selected at the first meeting of each school year. The secretary shall compile minutes in a notebook for each school year.

Open Chair

The first 15 minutes of each meeting will be designated as open chair. Any parent or staff member may address the Council to briefly state their opinions or concerns. The Council or a member designee will respond in writing to expressed concerns, if warranted, before the next meeting. A copy of the response(s) will become a part of the agenda/package distributed to each member at least two weeks prior to next meeting.

Subcommittees

To encourage productivity, subcommittees will be utilized to involve as many staff/parents as possible who are not serving on the Council and to assist in accomplishing the tasks of the Council.

Chapter 9

School Plan and School Budget

The primary responsibility of the site committee is to develop the annual school plan and its accompanying annual school budget. The annual school plan provides an operating structure for the school for the coming school year, while the annual school budget shows how funds will be spent to carry out this plan. Both the plan and the budget should be displayed in a manner that is easily understood by parents, students, and others not familiar with such documents. Once approved, the plan and the budget should be carried out as published, unless changes have also been approved. All school plans and budgets should be public and available to anyone interested in reviewing them.

In developing the annual school plan and budget, the site committee should review the following suggestions.

The School Plan and Budget Must Fit In with the Planning and Budget Cycles of the School System

The local school plan cannot be started until the local school has been informed of goals set by the school board and the superintendent. For example, if one of the board goals is to have at least 90% of the students reading at or above grade level, the local schools must know this far enough in advance to incorporate this goal into their plans. Similarly, the local schools must have an estimate of their allocations far enough in advance to develop budgets for their school plans. It is the superintendent's job to develop planning and budget cycles which will allow the school system to progress in an orderly manner. This is not a difficult task, but it is very important that it be done correctly. See the chapter on "Student Allocation of Funds" (Chapter Ten) for more details on this.

The School Plan Should Clearly Describe What Will Be Happening in the School During the Coming School Year

Although the plan should not include routine management operations (for example, how the cafeteria floor is cleaned), it should describe the major program activities of the schools, especially those that deviate from routine.

For example, later in this chapter is an extract from a high school plan which describes the development of a volunteer program. This was a new program for that school, made possible by the presence of school based management. In addition to descriptions of new programs in that school, the school plan describes a number of continuing and regular programs, such as improvement in student reading ability, because some new approaches were being used. This school plan, however, does not include any descriptions of programs which are permanent, unchanging parts of the school's operation. For example, the plan does not describe the guidance and counseling program. For the most part, then, the school plan should concentrate on the new and revised activities of the school which the presence of school based management has brought about. If every aspect of the school operation were included in the annual school plan, it would be a very cumbersome document and important innovations might be buried within it.

Permanent programs of the school (for example, football) are usually already known to the school community and are advertised in different ways. Furthermore, the annual school budget provides insight into the regular activities of the school by showing the various amounts of money being spent on these activities.

Having said this, however, it's up to the school system to decide how comprehensive the school plans should be.

The Format of School Plans Should Be Standardized

This suggestion is especially true in school systems where there are more than a few schools. If all schools are allowed to submit plans in different formats, it becomes burdensome for the superintendent to review them, complicated to compare one school with another, and difficult to determine if schools are pursuing school board goals.

A suggested format for the school plan can be seen in the extract of a school plan contained at the end of this chapter. But regardless of the actual format, each section of the plan should contain certain essential information:

- *What is the problem?* This section should clearly describe the problem which is being addressed.

- *What is the proposed solution to the problem?* This section should briefly address how the problem will be solved.

- *An analysis of the problem.* This section describes why the problem exists, and what impact the problem is having on the school.

- *The operational plan for the solution.* This is where the reader can find out just how the problem will be approached. It provides a time line, tasks that need to be accomplished, a designation of who does what, and what resources are needed.

- *How the project will be evaluated.* Every project in the school plan must include provisions for evaluation. This evaluation should be results-based and should describe exactly how well the problem was solved.

- *The cost of the project.* Every program described in the annual school plan should include a breakdown of costs. This way, there is no doubt about the exact cost of the project.

Although the school budget contains all projected school spending, a school budget does not always clearly show the exact cost of a single program within the school. That's why it's important to include the cost of the specific program in the plan itself.

The Annual School Plan and Budget Must Be Approved

Before it is carried out, the school plan must be approved by the superintendent; and before any funds can be spent by the local school, the school budget must be approved by both the superintendent and the school board. It is not necessary or recommended, however, that the school board approve school plans, as this would entrench the board deeply into the day-to-day operations of the schools. Also, if the board approved each individual school plan, members would become partly accountable for plan failures. However, the superintendent should present the school plans to the board for review before approving them. The board should study and discuss the plans with the superintendent. It is then up to the superintendent to weigh any advice of the board before taking action to approve or disapprove the plans.

Approved Budgets Should Not Be Changed

Although school plans and school budgets are not fixed, binding documents, they are the best description of what a school *plans* to do and how a school *plans* to spend its funds. Unless there are unexpected and uncontrollable events which could not reasonably have been provided for, the plans and budgets should be observed. However, should there be good cause for change in the school plan and/or budget, the superintendent should have an open mind. For example, if a school receives an unexpected donation, it might be wise and necessary to revise the school's plan and budget. The suggestion that schools should observe their plans and budgets does not mean that a local school should not be authorized to transfer school funds from one account to another within permissible limits. The school principal should be free within the law and sound financial management practices to transfer funds within the school for good cause. This discretion, though, does not relieve the school from following its plan or from explaining why transfers are made, or from seeking prior approval when required. Neither the school plan nor school budget should keep the school from meeting the legitimate educational needs of the school community.

The following sample extract from a comprehensive school plan developed by Woodbridge High School, Prince William County Schools, Virginia, is only one of many contained in the plan. Other topics included: conservation of the cost of utilities, after-school help for advanced placement students, improvement of the library/media center, in-school staff development, expansion in the role of department chairpersons, improvement of reading and writing skills, development of a prevention program for "at-risk" students, expansion of telephone service, and other programs designed to improve student learning. This plan was developed by extensive collaboration among students, staff, parents, and the principal.

A Sample School Plan Extract

A. The Problem:

There are many individuals in the community who are able to contribute to the education of our students. In an effort to better utilize this valuable educational resource, the school effectiveness team plans to implement a volunteer program.

Currently, there are hundreds of parents who volunteer many hours of service to the school. They perform numerous tasks and share in a myriad of responsibilities. However, there is not a plan in place to expand the volunteer program to maximize impact in the classroom or to guarantee that efforts from volunteers are appreciated by staff, students, and the community in general.

B. The Proposed Solution:

It is proposed that Woodbridge Senior High School develop a comprehensive volunteer program.

C. Analysis:

In order to provide a meaningful volunteer program for the purpose of maximizing the impact in the classroom, a teacher coordinator will organize volunteer teams for the various curricular and office areas. The teams will be called upon to formalize the volunteer program to include, but not be limited to the following: guest speakers, remedial tutorial assistance, assistance in the computer lab and library, clerical assistance, assistance in career counseling, assistance in standardized testing, and in other areas as needs arise.

D. Operational Plan:

1. Objective

    To develop a school-wide volunteer program.

2. Implementation Strategy

    a. During the spring of 1989, funding for this program will be identified by the principal. A supplement will be allocated. Funding for clerical services will be budgeted.

    b. A complete volunteer program will be in place at the beginning of the 1989-90 school year.

    c. The program will consist of the following elements:

    1) A teacher coordinator with supplement and released time from supervision

    2) A clerical assistant

    3) A monthly newsletter to staff and community

    4) A volunteer directory

    5) A recognition procedure

    6) Inter- and intra-departmental communication

7) Appointment of a community, parent volunteer coordinator

3. Responsibilities

    The responsibility for implementing the volunteer program will be assumed by the principal.

4. Evaluation

    The success of this program will be based upon the school having a successful volunteer program by the start of the 1989-90 school year.

    Success will mean that volunteers will be included in the following areas of operation:

    a. Instructional presentations in each department by each teacher

    b. Clerical assistants in each department and in administrative offices

    c. Career Center operation

    d. Extra-curricular coordination and supervision (field trips, chaperoning)

    e. Membership in all parent volunteer groups will increase by 20%

    f. Membership in the PSO will exceed 1100 paid members

    Success will also be indicated if a majority of parents, staff, and community members respond positively on a survey to be conducted by school administrators during the 1989-90 school year.

5. Cost

    The cost to Woodbridge Senior High School will be as follows:

    a. The cost of one supplement to pay a teacher who will be responsible for program coordination will be $1,000.

    b. The cost for supplies, equipment, phone tolls, etc., will be $100.

The total cost for implementing this recommendation will be $1,100.

SAMPLE SCHOOL BUDGET UNDER SCHOOL BASED MANAGEMENT

	FY 90 Approved Budget	POS	FY 91 Approved Budget	POS	Increase/(decrease) Budget	POS
Sample Middle School						
Principal	0	0.0	61,000	1.0	61,000	1.0
Asst Principal	0	0.0	49,300	1.0	49,300	1.0
Tchr, Adm Assgnmnt	0	0.0	33,700	1.0	33,700	1.0
Teacher, Classroom	0	0.0	1,875,400	55.4	1,875,400	55.4
Librarian	0	0.0	34,500	1.0	45,500	1.0
Counselor	0	0.0	107,700	3.0	107,700	3.0
Teacher Assistant	0	0.0	70,500	5.0	70,500	5.0
Sectl/Clerical	0	0.0	109.600	5.0	109,600	5.0
Custodian	0	0.0	110,000	5.5	110,000	5.5
Overtime	0	0.0	1,000	0.0	1,000	0.0
Temporary Employee	0	0.0	1,500	0.0	1,500	0.0
Substitute Teacher	0	0.0	24,703	0.0	24,703	0.0
Coaching Supplement	0	0.0	21,552	0.0	21,552	0.0
Extra-curr Supplement	0	0.0	6,928	0.0	6,928	0.0
Travel Reimbursement	0	0.0	2,473	0.0	2,473	0.0
Conf Expenses	0	0.0	1,500	0.0	1,500	0.0
Field Trips	0	0.0	5,716	0.0	5,716	0.0

Maintenance-Bldg	0	0.0	2,351	0.0	2,351	0.0
In-service Expenses	0	0.0	1,500	0.0	1,500	0.0
Office Supplies	0	0.0	10,203	0.0	10,203	0.0
Custodial Supplies	0	0.0	2,554	0.0	2,554	0.0
Instr Supplies	0	0.0	60,649	0.0	60,649	0.0
Library Periodicals	0	0.0	743	0.0	743	0.0
Equip/Furn, Add'l	0	0.0	22,386	0.0	22,386	0.0
Reserve/Contingency	0	0.0	13,833	0.0	13,833	0.0
	0	0.0	2,631,291	77.9	2,631,291	77.9

This sample middle school budget indicates that during the previous year, the school was not under school based management; therefore no funds were allocated to the school. However, the following year, the school shifted to school based management, and received an allotment of $2,631,291 for carrying out its responsibilities. Please note that POS refers to the average number per school of people in that position.

Chapter 10

Student Based Allocation of Funds

The two most important questions that a school system must answer when converting to school based management are:

- How much of the school system budget will be set aside for the schools?
- How will funds be allocated to the schools?

In answering these two questions, school systems should follow two guiding principles:

- There is a direct correlation between the amount of money set aside for the schools and the school system's commitment to school based management.
- All school based funds must be allocated on an *educationally fair basis*.

Unless the greatest share of the school system's operating budget is found in the schools, it is unlikely that a school system has real school based management. In the case of school management, money means power, and without money, the schools have little power. Therefore, a school system converting to school based management should attempt to transfer at least 75% of its operating budget to the schools, *along with the authority to use those funds*.

Funds should be distributed to the schools in a way that guarantees that each student receives *fair* share of the educational pie. This does not mean that each student receives an *equal* share of the pie. *When resources are distributed equally to students of unequal need, inequality is perpetuated. Equality of educational opportunity requires that while students needs are unequal, their needs attract equal attention and resources.*

How, then, does a school system go about transferring the greatest share of the operating budget to the schools equitably? This chapter will help you to determine which responsibilities should stay in the central office and which responsibilities (and accompanying funds) should go to the individual schools.

Existing System-Wide Average Salaries for Each Employee Classification

Under the model of school based management being discussed in this book, each school has funds for hiring staff assigned to the individual school. On the surface, this seems to create a serious fiscal inequity, since some school have expensive teachers (that is, those with advanced degrees and many years of experience), while other schools might have less expensive teachers (that is, those with no graduate degrees and with limited teaching experience). This seems to mean that while the one school would spend all of its money on teacher salaries, the other would have vast sums to spend on other needs and interests.

This apparent serious flaw is offset by charging schools the cost of the *average* employee salary. For example, while the actual salary being paid to a teacher in a given school might be $40,000, the school is only charged $35,000—the average salary for teachers system-wide. Or, while the actual salary being paid to a secretary might be $20,000, the school would be charged $23,000—the average salary of school secretaries system-wide. This neutralizes variations in employee costs due to experience, degree status, and salary classification. As a result, there is no advantage in hiring "cheap" teachers and no disadvantage in hiring "expensive" ones. A sample of average salaries is found later in this chapter.

Existing and Approved Program Staffing Ratios

Most school districts have guidelines on the size of classes and the number of students that may be assigned to a given teaching position.

For example, if each second grade class is assigned a teacher at a ration of 25 students to one teacher (25:1), then each second grade student, for purposes of fund allocation, is entitled to 1/25th of the teacher's average salary. If teachers for gifted and talented students are expected to carry an average student load of 60, for each gifted and talented student in the school the school receives 1/60th of the average salary of teachers. This process is repeated with each program in the school to determine the amount of money provided to the school for *staffing* needs. Samples of staffing ratios are found in this chapter.

Existing and Approved Funding Levels for Programs

Most school districts set aside money for certain programs based upon years of experience. For example, a school district may have found that the average for elementary textbooks works out to be $30 per child, while the average amount of money needed for elementary instructional supplies works out to be $40 per child. The school district, then, must decide what *non-staff* costs will be borne by the schools, and compute the average per pupil costs for those non-staff items. Some of the obvious non-staff items which should be considered for being school based are administrative supplies, custodial supplies, textbooks, library books, media materials, materials and equipment (instructional, administrative, and custodial), maintenance of non-standard equipment, routine and minor building maintenance, student field trips, school based staff development, and pay for temporary employees. All of these non-staff costs, when added together and divided by the total number of students in the school system, might work out to range from $200 to $800 per student, but since students have varying needs, a way must be found to assure that the school's allocation provides equitable funding for the different students actually enrolled in the school.

This is done by determining an **allocation factor**, or weighted factor, for each category of student, meaning, for example, that a special education student is weighted more heavily for allocation purposes than a student with no handicapping conditions or special needs. Since there is a direct relationship between staff and non-staff costs, the same weighted factor is used to determine both staff and non-staff allocations. Examples of staff and non-staff allocations are found later in this chapter.

One problem in developing a student based allocation of funds is that all schools, regardless of size, have certain fixed costs. For example, most school districts require that each school have a principal. If the average salary of a an elementary principal is $60,000, that salary takes a larger share of a small school's budget than of a large school's budget. All schools can be put on an "even playing field". This is done by giving each school a "fixed" allocation so that no school is rewarded or punished solely because of small size. This fixed amount gives each elementary, middle, high, and special school the money it needs to acquire staff and resources. An example of how fixed allocations are derived is found later in this chapter.

To fully understand this allocation procedure, it is important to remember that *the money follows the student.* In other words, every student in the school brings an individual financial allotment to the school based upon the needs of that student. For example, a second grade student with no handicaps or special needs might bring $3,000 to the school, while a low-income student with severe handicaps might bring $10,000 to the school. All of the varying amounts for each student are totalled into a *lump sum*, and that is the total amount of money available to run the school for the coming school year, according to an approved annual school plan and approved annual school budget.

Through this procedure, two middle schools, each with 1,000 students, might receive different sums of money, if for example one of the schools has more students with handicaps and/or special needs. A sample of how students are grouped for allocation purposes is found later in this chapter.

Most superintendents include a "reserve" fund in their budgets, because unforseen and uncontrollable costs are commonplace. Under school based management, there is a special need for a reserve fund, since "the money follows the student". If a school budget is based upon the prediction that 500 students will enroll, and 530 students actually enroll, the principal needs additional funds to educate these unanticipated students. A superintendent working under school based management would be able to transfer money for these additional thirty. With proper forecasting, however, this should occur rarely.

In discussions of budgeting for school based management, a number of questions may arise. Some are discussed here.

Can a School Carry Over Money from Year to Year?

Principals are often interested in knowing what happens if they don't spend all of the money allotted to them. Naturally, they would like to carry it over to the next year. This is acceptable *if* the law and local ground rules permit it. Frankly, however, principals should be held accountable for spending all funds allotted to them and should not be allowed to carry funds over to the next year, unless the carry-over is part of the approved school plan. For example, it is possible that a school might want to make a purchase (such as new foreign language laboratory) which it cannot pay for in one year. The superintendent could approve a carry-over of funds for a year or two, until the school has accumulated enough money to make the purchase.

What Happens if a School Spends More Than Its Allotted Budget?

This is a question which principals particularly would be concerned with. In converting to school based management, all principals need adequate training, especially in matters of budget management. They need to learn that they are expected not to overspend. If a school does overspend, it should be dealt with as would any other comparable situation. The reason for the excessive spending should be identified and appropriate action taken. If the reason was beyond the control of the principal and could not reasonably have been predicted, then the solution could be either to transfer money from the superintendent's reserve fund, or to retrieve the overspent funds from the school's budget for the ensuing school year.

Can Principals Transfer Funds within the Approved School Budget?

Budgets are not fixed, binding documents. They are supposed to be a *plan* for how money is to be spent. But recognizing that no one can predict the future, it is common practice to modify budgets as circumstances change. As a matter of fact, the principal should be given great freedom under law and sound accounting practices to transfer money for good cause. For example, if a principal finds that less money is needed for cleaning supplies than anticipated, but that more money is needed for textbooks, the principal should be allowed to make that transfer. To what extent prior permission is required for such a transfer is a matter for each school system to decide.

Although a budget is merely a plan and principals should be allowed to make transfers, that does not mean that a school should be allowed to deviate significantly from its approved school plan. For example, if a school plan calls for the hiring of two extra part-time cafeteria aides, and the principal uses the money not to hire aides, but to purchase computers, the principal owes his or her supervisor a very good explanation. School based management does not give schools license to spend as they choose. Spending should be according to the plan, and the central office should be organized so that it can monitor all school spending.

What Happens if the School System Revenues Are Less Than Called For in the Budget?

It is not uncommon for school districts to face this problem. Tax revenues may be less than planned for or the state might cut back on school funding. In such cases, a school district must cut back or "freeze" spending in certain areas. When this happens under school based management (keeping in mind that over 75% of the budget may be in the schools), the superintendent determines the size of the problem and then imposes a percentage reduction in each school's budget.

Under a centralized budget system based upon programs rather than schools, the superintendent decides which programs will face reduction or termination. Under school based management, each school makes its own decision as to how to reduce its budget. This is preferable to having the superintendent tell each school what must be cut from the school's budget, because the superintendent is not close enough to the schools to know how best to make cuts. The school principal and other stakeholders in the school are in a better the position to determine what cuts should be made.

Can Schools Purchase Directly from the Private Sector?

Yes, but they must follow all proper purchasing procedures. Experience has shown, however, that most principals continue to purchase through the central office.

An anecdote shows the benefit of local school control over spending. A school principal in a suburban school district received a kiln from the art supervisor to be used in the art class. For *three years* the principal put in work orders to have the kiln connected for use, but his work orders were of very low priority when they were received in the central office. When that school converted to school based management, the principal then had funds for equipment and minor repair and maintenance. He made one final request to the central office to have the kiln wired for use and the request was again ignored. The principal then contacted a local electrician on a Friday. The electrician installed the kiln over the weekend and the students used it on Monday. When the central office maintenance crew heard about this, they were quite upset and threatened. From that point on, the central office maintenance crew became much more sensitive to the work orders from the schools.

If Each School Makes Its Own Purchases, Are the Economies of Bulk Purchasing Lost?

Obviously, duplicating paper bought by the truck load is less expensive than duplicating paper purchased one ream at a time at the local stationery store. Under school based management each principal decides how much paper is needed for the year and then sends a purchase order to the central office, where all such school orders are combined and one large order is placed for duplicating paper. When the paper arrives, it is distributed according to the requests made by the schools. This same practice can be applied to professional journals, library books, textbooks, instructional equipment, instructional supplies, etc.

Does the School Based Management Budget Process Put More Work on the Principals?

Yes—at the outset. After that, the principal should work no harder, but will work smarter. During the first two years of school based management, the principals will find that budget development and administration require more work. However, with proper training before the conversion is made, this extra work should be minimal. Good training on budget-related matters can be provided in two days. After the principals master the concepts of school based management, they generally feel more satisfied and competent.

Is the Allocation Process 100% Fair?

No. The allocation process described in this book is about as good as it can get, but it is not perfect. For example, some schools will spend more than others on textbooks, while some schools will spend more than others on cleaning supplies. However, when all of the spending of the schools is totaled and averaged, each school should be very equitable. But remember, even if there are minor inequities, these also exist in a highly centralized management structure. Therefore, school based management should not be withheld because of minor inequities.

If a School Is Paying Its Own Utilities, Can It Keep Its Savings?

Yes, definitely. If a school can save money through energy conservation, it should be allowed to retain that money and apply it above and beyond the allocation for next year. If a school board were to take this money away from the school, it would discourage other schools from trying to save money, and would eliminate funds that probably would go to creative and innovative programs.

For example, in a large high school under school based management, the annual utility cost was about $400,000. The following year under school based management the utility bill was reduced to about $360,000. The principal (with agreement from the site committee) invested the $40,000 savings in the school's media center by installing a bank of computers for student use. As a result of those savings, the school now has one of best media centers in the area.

What Does the Published School System Budget Look Like under School Based Management?

Basically, the budget looks the same, except it now contains an extra budget page for each school in the school system. Under a "program" budget, it is easy to see how much money is being spent on math, but it is difficult to determine how much money is being spent in each school. A school based management budget has both program budgets (that is, those left in the central office) and complete budgets for each school showing exactly how that school is spending money. Some professionals feel that this method of school based management budget display provides superior insight into exactly how funds are being spent. Certainly, it assures a greater balance of resources among the schools. Examples of school budgets and central office budgets appear later in this chapter.

Must the Amount of Money Allocated to Each Student Category Actually Be Spent on Each Student in That Category?

In other words, if $1,796 is allocated to Level 1 students (that is, regular students with no special needs), must $1,796 actually be spent on each such student? No. Even in the case of special education, no fixed amount of money must be spent. The only requirement is that spending meets all legal requirements, such as the IEP (Individualized Education Program) in special education.

The Allocation Process

Under this model of school based management, each school receives money for its annual budget from two sources:

- *FIXED ALLOCATION,* which is designed to provide a base allocation to put all schools on a "level playing field", regardless of size
- *PER PUPIL ALLOCATION,* which is based upon the nature of the student

The *FIXED ALLOCATION* is for personnel and resources that are the same for all schools regardless of enrollment. For example, most school districts require a principal for each school. Other common requirement among all schools might also include:

- A reading teacher
- A librarian
- Baseline staffing

- Extra-curricular supplements
- Athletic field trips

The *PER PUPIL ALLOCATION* is based upon what category each student is placed in. This allocation covers all school staff and non-staff needs, such as supplies, equipment, services, substitutes, and some maintenance.

SAMPLE FIXED ALLOCATIONS*
(For Demonstration ONLY)

Elementary Schools: $272,500

    1.0 Principal
    1.0 Librarian
    1.0 Reading Teacher
    1.0 Guidance Counselor
    2.5 Secretaries
    1.5 Custodians
    1.0 Cafeteria Aide
        Extra-Curricular Supplements

Middle Schools: $309,200

    1.0 Principal
    1.0 Librarian
    1.0 Reading Teacher
    4.0 Secretaries
    1.5 Custodians
        Athletic Field Trips
        Extra-Curricular Supplements

High Schools: $759,400

    1.0 Principal
    1.0 Librarian
    1.0 Reading Teacher
    1.0 Director of Student Activities
    1.0 Guidance Director
    1.0 Career Counselor
    1.0 Vocational Resource Teacher
    1.0 ISS Teacher & Aide
    7.0 Secretaries

---

* Under the plan described in this book, each school would be free to spend its allocation as it sees fit, within set limits. In other words, if not in violation of a requirement, an elementary school could elect not to use a reading teacher, but the school would keep the money for some other application.

1.5 Custodians
2.0 Security Specialists
　　 Athletic Field Trips
　　 Extra-Curricular Supplements

Special Schools: $192,700

1.0 Principal
1.0 School Nurse
0.5 Adapted P.E. Teacher
1.5 Secretaries
1.5 Custodians

SAMPLE STAFFING RATIOS*
(For Demonstration ONLY)

ELEMENTARY SCHOOL	SAMPLE STAFFING RATIO
Kindergarten	AVG = 25:1 MAX = 30:1 Aide with all classes
Grade 1	AVG = 24:1 MAX = 30:1
Grades 2-3	AVG = 25:1 MAX = 30:1
Grades 4-5	AVG = 25:1 MAX = 30:1
Reading	1 full-time
Art/Music/PE	AVG = 960 students per week MAX = 1,000 students per week
Strings	AVG = 15:1 MAX = 25:1
Chapter I	AVG = 40:1 MAX = 45:1
ESL	AVG = 15:1 without aide 25:1 with aide
Gifted & Talented	AVG = 60:1 MAX = 75:1
Principal	1 full-time
Assistant Principal	1 full-time each 575
Librarian	1 full-time

---

* Staffing ratios must be established to determine how much money is needed by each school for *staffing purposes.*

Guidance Counselors	1 full-time to 550 1 add'l half-time at 550 1 add'l half-time at 750 1 add'l half-time at 950
Secretary	1 full-time library 1.5 full-time office to 650 1 add'l half-time at 650
Cafeteria Aide	Part-time per school

SAMPLE STAFFING RATIOS
(For Demonstration ONLY)

MIDDLE SCHOOL	SAMPLE STAFFING RATIO
Grade 6	AVG = 24:1 MAX = 30:1
Art	AVG = 110 students per day MAX = 20 students per class
Foreign Language	AVG = 22:1 MAX = 30:1
Health & P.E.	AVG = 32:1 MAX = 40:1
Home Economics	AVG = 110 students per day MAX = 20 students per class
Language Arts	AVG = 24:1 MAX = 30:1
Mathematics	AVG = 25:1 MAX = 30:1
Music	AVG = 30:1 MAX = 1,000 students per week
Science	AVG = 25:1 MAX = 30:1
Social Studies	AVG = 25:1 MAX = 30:1
Technology Education	AVG = 110 students per day MAX = 20 students per class
Reading	1 full-time
ESL	AVG = 15:1 without aide 25:1 with aide

Gifted & Talented	AVG = 120:1 MAX = 150:1
Principal	1 full-time
Assistant Principal	1 full-time each 575
Librarian	1 full-time to 1,000 1 add'l full-time at 1,000
Guidance Counselors	1 full-time to 440 1 add'l full-time at 440 1 add'l full-time at 840 1 add'l full time at 1,240
Secretary	1 full-time library 4 full-time office to 1,400 1 add'l full-time office at 11,400

SAMPLE STAFFING RATIOS
(For Demonstration ONLY)

HIGH SCHOOL	SAMPLE STAFFING RATIO
Art	AVG = 20:1 MAX = 30:1
Business Ed	AVG = 18:1 MAX = 25:1
Foreign Language	AVG = 22:1 MAX = 30:1
Health & P.E.	AVG = 32:1 MAX = 40:1
Home Economics	AVG = 18:1 MAX = 20:1
ICT	MAX = 20:1
Language Arts	AVG = 24:1 MAX = 30:1
Marketing Ed	MAX = 20:1
Mathematics	AVG = 23:1 MAX = 30:1
Music	AVG = 25:1 MAX = 1,000 students per week
Science	AVG = 23:1 MAX = 30:1
Social Studies	AVG = 25:1 MAX = 30:1
Technology Education	AVG = 18:1 MAX = 20:1
Trade & Industry	AVG = 18:1 MAX = 20:1

Reading	AVG = 40:1
	MAX = 45:1
Drivers Ed	AVG = 240:1
	MAX = 265:1
ESL	AVG = 15:1 without aide
	25:1 with aide
Gifted & Talented	AVG = 120:1
	MAX = 150:1
Principal	1 full-time
Assistant Principal	1 full-time each 575
Librarian	1 full-time to 1,000
	1 add'l full-time at 1,000
	1 add'l full-time at 2,000
Guidance Counselors	1 full-time to 385
	1 add'l full-time each 350 above 385
	1 career counselor
	1 guidance counselor
Secretary	1 full-time library to 2,000
	1 add'l full-time library at 2,000
	7 full-time to 800
	2 add'l full-time at 1400
	1 add'l full-time each 600 above 1400

SAMPLE STAFFING RATIOS
(For Demonstration ONLY)

SPECIAL EDUCATION	SAMPLE STAFFING RATIO
ED Resource	MAX = 24:1
EDSC	MAX = 8:1 without aide 10:1 with aide
EMR (Grades 1-3)	MAX = 9:1 without aide 11:1 with aide
EMR (Grades 4-8)	MAX = 10:1 without aide 134:1 with aide
EMR (Grades 9-12)	MAX = 17:1
Hearing Impaired	MAX = 8:1 without aide 10:1 with aide
HI Resource	MAX = 24:1
LD Resource	MAX = 24:1
LDSC	MAX = 8:1 without aide 10:1 with aide
Occupational Therapist	AVG = 20:1
Physically Handicapped	MAX = 8:1 without aide 10:1 with aide
Physical Therapist	AVG = 30:1
Pre-School Center-Based	MAX = 8:1 with aide
Pre-School Home-Based	MAX = 12:1
Severe & Profound	MAX = 6:1 without aide 8:1 with aide
Speech & Language	MAX = 75:1
TMR	MAX = 8:1 without aide 10:1 with aide

AVERAGE SALARIES*
(For Demonstration ONLY)

POSITION	CONTRACT LENGTH (Days)	AVERAGE SALARY
Assistant Principal, Elementary	223	$44,200
Assistant Principal, Middle	223	$49,300
Assistant Principal, High	236	$52,700
Bookkeeper	223	$24,000
Building Engineer	250	$28,900
Cafeteria Aide	184	$ 2,800
Custodian	250	$20,000
Director Student Activities	210	$36,500
Executive Secretary I	250	$33,200
Guidance Counselor, Elementary	194	$33,700
Guidance Counselor, Middle	199	$34,500
Guidance Counselor, High	199	$34,500
Guidance Director, Middle	223	$38,700
Guidance Director, High	223	$38,700
Librarian	199	$34,500
Office Assistant	194	$13,000
Office Assistant	250	$16,700
Principal, Elementary	250	$59,200

---

*The average salary of all positions assigned to the schools must be determined so that each school budget is charged the average salary for each position, regardless of the actual salary being earned. This assures that no school gains or loses because of the actual salaries being paid.

Principal, Middle	250	$61,000
Principal, High	250	$68,000
Principal, Special	250	$57,000
School Nurse	194	$33,700
Secretary I	200	$17,300
Secretary II	200	$18,600
Secretary II	223	$20,700
Secretary III	223	$24,000
Secretary III	250	$26,900
School Safety & Security Officer	250	$33,200
Student Attendant	184	$11,500
Teacher	194	$33,700
Teacher	199	$34,500
Teacher	214	$37,100
Teacher	223	$38,700
Teacher Assistant	188	$14,100

SAMPLE PER PUPIL STAFF ALLOCATION
GRADES 1-5*
(For Demonstration ONLY)

Required Staff	Staff Ratio	Factor	X	Salary	=	Per Pupil
Regular Teacher	25	0.0400		$33,700		$1,348
Art Teacher	850	0.0012		$33,700		$40
Music Teacher	850	0.0012		$33,700		$40
P.E. Teacher	850	0.0012		$33,700		$40
Assistant Principal	575	0.0017		$44,200		$75
Guidance Counselor	1050	0.0010		$33,700		$33
Secretary	625	0.0016		$18,600		$29
Custodian	340	0.0029		$20,000		$58

---

*This table shows how much staff salary is set aside for each regular student in grades 1–5, based upon average salaries.

SAMPLE PER PUPIL STAFF ALLOCATION
(For Demonstration ONLY)

ALLOCATION CATEGORY	FACTOR	PER PUPIL
Level 1	0.67*	$ 1,112
Kindergarten		
Level 2	1.00	1,660
Grades 1-5		
Level 3	1.43	2,374
Grades 6-12		
Transitional-1		
Level 4	1.64	2,722
Vocational		
Level 5	1.99	3,303
EMR (9-12)		
Pre-School (Home)		
Level 6	2.93	4,864
EMR (K-8)		
Level 7	3.54	5,876
EDSC		
LCSC		
Pre-School (Center)		
Level 8	4.09	6,789
Hearing Impaired		
Orthopedic Impaired		
TMR		
Level 9	5.28	8,765
Severe & Profound		

---

*In this and all other examples, an allocation factor of 1.00 has been assigned to Level 2 (Grades 1-5) students. All other factors and costs are determined in relation to these Level 2 students.

Level 10	5.31	8,815
ED (PACE)		
ALLOCATION CATEGORY	**FACTOR**	**PER PUPIL**
Resource		
Econ. Disadvantaged	0.07	$ 116
ED Resource	1.27	2,108
ESL	1.30	2,158
Gifted & Talented (K-5)	0.29	481
Gifted & Talented (6-12)	0.18	299
Hearing Resource	1.89	3,137
LD Resource	0.97	1,610
Occup. Therapist	0.81	1,345
Physical Therapist	0.68	1,129
Speech & Language	0.37	614
Vision Resource	1.89	3,137
Fixed Allocation		
Elementary School		272,500
Middle School		309,200
High School		759,400
Special School		192,700

SAMPLE STUDENT ENROLLMENT
(For Demonstration ONLY)

CATEGORY	FACTOR	X STUDENTS	=	WEIGHTED* STUDENTS
Level 1 Kindergarten	0.67	3,323		2,226
Level 2 Grades 1-5	1.00	16,320		16,320
Level 3 Grades 6-12 Transitional-1	1.43	19,825		28,350
Level 4 Trade & Industry	1.64	814		1,335
Level 5 EMR (9-12) Pre-School (Home)	1.99	245		488
Level 6 EMR (K-8)	2.93	102		299
Level 7 EDSC LDSC Pre-School (Center)	3.54	1,084		3,837
Level 8 Hearing Impaired Orthopedic Impaired TMR	4.09	209		855

---

*In this hypothetical school system, there are 42,027 students. However, when their special needs are considered, these 42,027 students are the equivalent of 57,974 regular elementary (Level 2) students.

Level 9 Severe & Profound	5.28	80	422
Level 10 ED (PACE)	5.31	25	133
Resource			
Econ. Disadvantaged	0.07	2,808	197
ED Resource	1.27	80	102
ESL	1.30	178	231
G/T (K-5)	0.29	790	229
G/T (6-12)	0.18	1,099	198
Hearing Resource	1.89	36	68
LD Resource	0.97	1,471	1,427
Occup. Therapist	0.81	300	243
Physical Therapist	0.68	204	139
Speech & Language	0.37	2,131	788
Vision Resource	1.89	46	87
Total		42,027	57,974

SUPPLIES, EQUIPMENT & SERVICES*
(For Demonstration ONLY)

DESCRIPTION	FUNDS AVAILABLE	BASIC ALLOCATION
Equipment & Furniture	$1,990,329	$ 34.33
Field Trips	136,800	2.36
Instructional Materials	1,740,748	30.03
Library Materials	415,179	7.16
Maintenance	100,000	1.72
Non-Instr. Material	434,282	7.49
Staff Development	168,186	2.90
Substitute Teachers	858,320	14.81
Temp. Empl. & Overtime	359.462	6.20
Textbooks	1,700,000	29.32
TOTAL	**$7,903,306**	**$136.33**

*In this hypothetical school district of approximately 42,000 students, these are the amounts of non-staff funds set aside in certain categories identified for allocation to the schools. This table indicates that regular students in grades 1–5 (Level 2) would receive $136.33 each for non-staff needs. A Level 10 student would receive $723.91.

SAMPLE PER PUPIL NON-STAFF ALLOCATION*
(For Demonstration ONLY)

CATEGORY	FACTOR	PER PUPIL
Level 1 Kindergarten	0.67	91.34
Level 2 Grades 1-5	1.00	136.33
Level 3 Grades 6-12 Transitional-1	1.43	194.95
Level 4 Vocational	1.64	223.58
Level 5 EMR (9-12) Pre-School (Home)	1.99	271.30
Level 6 EMR (K-8)	2.93	399.45
Level 7 EDSC LDSC Pre-School (Center)	3.54	482.61
Level 8 Hearing Impaired Orthopedic Impaired TMR	4.09	557.59
Level 9 Severe & Profound	5.28	719.82

*This table shows how students assigned to different categories receive varying amounts of money for non-staff purposes.

Level 10	5.31	723.91
ED (PACE)		
Resource		
Econ. Disadvantaged	0.07	9.54
ED Resource	1.27	173.14
ESL	1.30	177.23
G/T (K-5)	0.29	39.54
G/T (6-12)	0.18	24.54
Hearing Resource	1.89	257.66
LD Resource	0.97	132.24
Occup. Therapist	0.81	110.43
Physical Therapist	0.68	92.70
Speech & Language	0.37	50.44
Vision Resource	1.89	257.66

SAMPLE PER PUPIL ALLOCATION FACTORS*
(For Demonstration ONLY)

ALLOCATION CATEGORY	FACTOR	STAFF	NON-STAFF	TOTAL
Level 1 Kindergarten	0.67	$1,112	$91.34	$1,203
Level 2 Grades 1-5	1.00	1,660	136.33	1,796
Level 3 Grades 6-12 Transitional-1	1.43	2,374	194.95	2,569
Level 4 Vocational	1.64	2,722	223.58	2,946
Level 5 EMR (9-12) Pre-School (Home)	1.99	3,303	271.30	3,574
Level 6 EMR (K-8)	2.93	4,864	399.45	5,263
Level 7 EDSC LDSC Pre-School (Center)	3.54	5,876	482.61	6,359
Level 8 Hearing Impaired Orthopedic Impaired TMR	4.09	6,789	557.59	7,347
Level 9 Severe & Profound	5.28	8,765	719.82	9,485

*This table combines staff and non-staff allocations.

Level 10	5.31	8,815	723.91	9,539
ED (PACE)				
Resource				
Econ. Disadvantaged	0.07	116	9.54	126
ED Resource	1.27	2,108	173.14	2,281
ESL	1.30	2,158	177.23	2,335
G/T (K-5)	0.29	481	39.54	521
G/T (6-12	0.18	299	24.54	324
Hearing Resource	1.89	3,137	257.66	3,395
LD Resource	0.97	1,610	132.24	1,742
Occup. Therapist	0.81	1,345	110.43	1,455
Physical Therapist	0.68	1,129	92.70	1,222
Speech & Language	0.37	614	50.44	664
Vision Resource	1.89	3,137	257.66	3,395
Fixed Allocation				
Elementary School		$272,500		
Middle School		309,200		
High School		759,400		
Special School		192,700		

SAMPLE ELEMENTARY SCHOOL*
(For Demonstration ONLY)

SELF-CONTAINED PROGRAMS

PROGRAM	STUDENTS
Kindergarten	98
1st Grade	96
2nd Grade	103
3rd Grade	96
4th Grade	107
5th Grade	116
EDSC	10
LDSC	11
TOTAL SELF-CONTAINED	**651**

RESOURCE PROGRAMS

PROGRAM	STUDENTS
Econ. Disadvantaged	49
Gifted & Talented	16
LD Resource	17
Speech & Language	63
TOTAL RESOURCE	**145**

*To determine budget allotments, each school must count the number of students that fall into each allocation category.

SAMPLE ELEMENTARY SCHOOL STAFFING COSTS*
(For Demonstration ONLY)

POSITION	NUMBER	X	SALARY	=	COST
Principal	1.0		$59,200		$59,200
Assistant Principal	1.0		44,200		44,200
Librarian	1.0		34,500		34,500
Guidance Counselor	1.5		33,700		50,550
Kindergarten Teachers	2.0		33,700		67,400
T-1 Teachers	1.0		33,700		33,700
1st Grade Teachers	4.0		33,700		134,800
2nd Grade Teachers	4.0		33,700		134,800
3rd Grade Teachers	4.0		33,700		134,800
4th Grade Teachers	4.0		33,700		134,800
5th Grade Teachers	5.0		33,700		168,500
Art Teacher	0.8		33,700		26,960
Music Teacher	1.0		33,700		33.700
P.E. Teacher	0.8		33,700		26,960
EDSC Teacher	1.0		33,700		33.700
LD Teachers	2.0		33,700		67,400
Speech Teacher	1.2		33,700		40,440
Reading Teacher	1.0		33,700		33,700

*To determine its staff costs, each school must count the number of staff members in each job category assigned to the school. In this case, the school is being charged $1,447,210 for staff salaries. This total is based on average salaries for the job classification.

Library Secretary	1.0	17,300	17,300
Office Secretary (200-day)	1.0	18,600	18,600
Office Secretary (223-day)	1.0	20,700	20,700
Custodians	3.0	20,000	60,000
Teacher Assistants	5.0	14,100	70,500
Total Staff Cost	**47.3**		**1,447,210**

CALCULATION SHEET*
(For Demonstration ONLY)

Allocation Category	Students	X	Per Pupil	=	Allocation
Level 1					
Kindergarten	98		1,203.34		$117,927
Level 2					
Grades 1-5	518		1,796.33		930,499
Level 3					
Grades 6-12	0		2,568.95		0
Transitional-1	14		2,568.95		35,965
Level 4					
Vocational	0		2,945.58		0
Level 5					
EMR (9-12)	0		3,574.30		0
Pre-School (Home)	0		3,574.30		0
Level 6					
EMR (K-8)	0		5,263.45		0
Level 7					
EDSC	10		6,358.61		63,586
LDSC	11		6,358.61		69,945
Pre-School (Center)	0		6,358.61		0
Level 8					
Hearing Impaired	0		7,346.59		0
Orthopedic Impaired	0		7,346.59		0

---

* Staff and non-staff allotments have been combined here to determine the total allotment to this school.

Student Based Allocation of Funds

TMR	0	7,346.59	0
Level 9			
Severe & Profound	0	9,484.82	0
Level 10			
ED (PACE)	0	9,538.91	0
Resource			
Economically Disadvantaged	49	125.54	6,151
ED Resource	0	2,281.14	0
ESL	0	2,335.23	0
Gifted & Talented (K-5)	16	520.54	8,329
Gifted & Talented (6-12)	0	323.54	0
Hearing Resource	0	3,394.66	0
LD Resource	17	1,742.24	29,618
Occupational Therapist	0	1,455.43	0
Physical Therapist	0	1,221.70	0
Speech & Language	63	664.44	41,860
Vision Resource	0	3,394.66	0
PER PUPIL ALLOCATION			**$1,303,880**
FIXED ALLOCATION			**$272,500**
TOTAL ALLOCATION			**$1,576,380**

SAMPLE ELEMENTARY SCHOOL BASED MANAGEMENT BUDGET
(For Demonstration ONLY)

Centerville Elem. School	Budget
Principal	59,200
Teacher, Classroom	899,790
Librarian	34,500
Counselor	33,700
Teacher Assistant	63,450
Cafeteria Aide	2,800
Secretarial/Clerical	47,300
Custodian	60,000
Overtime	1,200
Temporary Employee	920
Substitute Teacher	10,680
Substitute, Other	3,180
Excurr. Supplement	1,264
Travel Reimbursement	1,050
Conference Expenses	300
Field Trips	1,000
Maintenance—Bldg.	1,004
Printing/Duplicating	200
Postage	50
Educational TV	25
Office Supplies	2,000

Medical Supplies	50
Custodial Supplies	3,800
Reference Materials	700
Instructional Supplies	17,625
Library Books	2,360
Library Periodicals	490
Library Supplies	875
Equip./Furn., Add'l.	6,800
Reserve/Contingency	23,136
TOTAL	**1,279,449**

SAMPLE MIDDLE SCHOOL BASED MANAGEMENT BUDGET
(For Demonstration Only)

Jones Middle School	Budget
Principal	61,000
Asst. Principal	98,600
Teacher, Classroom	2,182,880
Librarian	34,500
Counselor	107,700
Teacher Assistant	70,500
Secretarial/Clerical	109,600
Custodian	140,000
Overtime	200
Substitute Teacher	19,554
Substitute, Other	3,809
Coaching Supplement	15,126
Excurr. Supplement	6,972
Consultant	1,000
Travel Reimbursement	3,556
Conference Expenses	2,000
Field Trips	4,150
Maintenance—Bldg.	3,651
In-service Expenses	349
Printing/Duplicating	8,500

Postage	2,200
Excurr. Expenses	1,200
Office Supplies	9,200
Medical Supplies	400
Custodial Supplies	7,000
Wearing Apparel	1,500
Excurr. Supplies	3,100
Instructional Supplies	47,281
Testing Materials	800
Library Books	6,650
Library Periodicals	850
Library Supplies	2,000
Equip./Furn., Add'l.	20,970
DP Equip., Add'l.	4,656
Equip./Furn, Repl.	7,500
TOTAL	**2,988,954**

SAMPLE HIGH SCHOOL BASED MANAGEMENT BUDGET
(For Demonstration ONLY)

Smith High School	Budget
Principal	68,000
Asst. Principal	263,500
Teacher, Auxiliary	0
Teacher, Admin. Assignment	70,200
Teacher, Classroom	5,859,820
Librarian	103,500
Counselor	383,700
Teacher Assistant	98,700
Specialist	47,200
Sec/Clerical	269,800
Maintenance Personnel	0
Custodian	360,000
Overtime	25,591
Temporary Employee	12,700
Substitute Teacher	63,330
Substitute, Other	1,000
Coaching Supplement	83,285
Excurr. Supplement	46,785
Other Salaries/Wages	0
Employee Benefits	0
Contractual Services	0
Consultant	500

Travel Reimbursement	9,735
Field Trips	27,205
Maintenance—Bldg.	2,444
Maintenance—Equip.	2,444
In-service Expenses	4,940
Printing/Duplicating	2,000
Postage	5,000
Excurr. Expenses	12,231
Educational TV	1,000
Rental Equipment	500
Materials & Supplies	0
Office Supplies	14,500
Medical Supplies	700
Custodial Supplies	17,900
Maintenance Supplies	4,944
Wearing Apparel	1,180
Reference Materials	4,085
Excurr. Supplies	4,490
Instructional Supplies	119,097
Textbooks	25,407
Testing Materials	9,869
Library Books	11,000
Library Periodicals	7,500
Library Supplies	2,440
Capital Outlay	0

Equip/Furn, Add'l	75,101
DP Equip, Add'l	26,167
Equip/Furn, Repl.	20,211
DP Equip, Repl.	1,200
Reserve/Contingency	0
TOTAL	**8,170,901**

SAMPLE CENTRAL OFFICE BUDGET UNDER SCHOOL BASED MANAGEMENT
(For Demonstration ONLY)

	FY 90 Approved Budget	POS	FY 91 Approved Budget	POS	Increase/(decrease) Budget	POS
Construction						
Supervisor	61,798	1.0	54,903	1.0	(6,895)	0.0
Project Manager	97,696	2.0	101,269	2.0	3,573	0.0
Sec/Clerical	29,747	1.0	31,532	1.0	1,785	0.0
Engineering Svcs	250,000	0.0	15,000	0.0	(235,000)	0.0
Travel Reimbursement	600	0.0	600	0.0	120	0.0
Office Supplies	1,400	0.0	2,250	0.0	850	0.0
Equip/Furn Add'l	500	0.0	0	0.0	(500)	0.0
Auto/Truck Add'l	0	0.0	0	0.0	0	0.0
Purchase of Land	0	0.0	0	0.0	0	0.0
Site Improvement	0	0.0	0	0.0	0	0.0
Building, New	0	0.0	0	0.0	0	0.0
Building, Addition	0	0.0	0	0.0	0	0.0
Building, Alteration	0	0.0	0	0.0	0	0.0
	441,741	4.0	205,554	4.0	(236,187)	0.0

This budget is an example of a central office budget which is not affected by school based management. The construction of new school buildings is clearly an example of a budget responsibility which should be retained in the central office. POS refers to the number of people filling that position.

SAMPLE CENTRAL OFFICE BUDGET UNDER SCHOOL BASED MANAGEMENT
(For Demonstration ONLY)

	FY 90 Approved Budget	POS	FY 91 Approved Budget	POS	Increase/(Decrease) Budget	POS
Elementary Education						
Director	71,073	1.0	0	0.0	(71,073)	(1.0)
Supervisor	55,395	1.0	0	0.0	(55,395)	(1.0)
Principal	1,992,387	33.5	0	0.0	(1,992,387)	(33.5)
Asst Principal	751,214	17.0	0	0.0	(751,214)	(17.0)
Tchr Classroom	22,429,909	688.5	0	0.0	(22,429,909)	(688.5)
Tchr Asst	839,757	59.5	0	0.0	(839,757)	(59.5)
Aides, Cafeteria	82,672	32.2	0	0.0	(82,672)	(32.0)
Sectl/Clerical	1,063,716	53.5	0	0.0	(1,063,716)	(53.5)
Overtime	2,544	0.0	0	0.0	(2,544)	0.0
Temp Employees	9,765	0.0	0	0.0	(9,765)	0.0
Sub/Other	14,038	0.0	0	0.0	(14,038)	0.0
Extra-curr Suppl	27,776	0.0	0	0.0	(27,776)	0.0
Conf Exp-admin	500	0.0	0	0.0	(500)	0.0
Travel Reimburse	22,762	0.0	0	0.0	(22,762)	0.0
In-serv Compnsn	6,801	0.0	0	0.0	(6,801)	0.0
Print/Dupl	2,400	0.0	0	0.0	(2,400)	0.0
Statnry/Prnt Fms	4,545	0.0	0	0.0	(4,545)	0.0
Instrctnal Supplies	120,000	0.0	0	0.0	(120,000)	0.0
Emp Trng-Supplies	0	0.0	0	0.0	0	0.0
In-serv/Supplies	287	0.0	0	0.0	(287)	0.0

Library Books	150,000	0.0	0	0.0	(125,787)	0.0
Equip/Furn, Addl	125,787	0.0	0		(125,787)	0.0
	27,773,658	886.0	0	0.0	(27,773,658)	(886.0)

This budget is an example of a central office budget which had large sums transferred from it to the budgets of the schools as a result of school based management. Prior to school based management, that is, prior to the FY 91 budget, the elementary program was financed and controlled from the central office. In FY 91, with the advent of school based management, that office was eliminated and the funds for teacher salaries, principal salaries, secretarial salaries, supplies, equipment, etc., were transferred to the individual school budgets.

SAMPLE CENTRAL OFFICE BUDGET UNDER SCHOOL BASED MANAGEMENT
(For Demonstration ONLY)

	FY 90 Approved Budget	POS	FY 91 Approved Budget	POS	Increase/(decrease) Budget	POS
Library Media Programs						
Supervisor	60,463	1.0	64,090	1.0	3,627	0.0
Librarian	2,033,098	55.5	14,635	0.5	(2,018,463)	(55.0)
Sec/Clerical	811,492	48.5	72,835	3.0	(738,657)	(45.5)
Sub/Other	7,500	0.0	0	0.0	(7,500)	0.0
Educatn Consult	180	0.0	0	0.0	120	0.0
Travel Reimburse	973	0.0	0	0.0	0	0.0
Conf Expense	0	0.0	200	0.0	200	0.0
In-serv Compnstn	300	0.0	2,100	0.0	1,800	0.0
Printing/Dupl	5,328	0.0	1,436	0.0	(3,892)	0.0
Rental/Equip	540	0.0	0	0.0	(540)	0.0
Other Contr Ser	2,000	0.0	0	0.0	(2,000)	0.0
Ref Material	4,500	0.0	2,205	0.0	(2,295)	0.0
Instr Supplies	0	0.0	0	0.0	0	0.0
Library Books	346,419	0.0	15,276	0.0	(331,143)	0.0
Library Periodicals	26,211	0.0	9,500	0.0	(16,711)	0.0
Library Supplies	32,697	0.0	0	0.0	(32,697)	0.0
Other Mtrls/Supps	1,550	0.0	0	0.0	(1,550)	0.0
Equip/furn Add'l	12,967	0.0	0	0.0	(12,967)	0.0
	3,346,218	105.0	183,550	4.5	(3,162,668)	(100.5)

This is a sample of a central office budget for library media programs. Because there was no school based management in this school system in FY 89 and FY 90, all library funds were retained in the central office. However, the following year the school system converted to school based management. Consequently, over $3,000,000 was transferred to the schools for incorporation into their budgets.

SAMPLE CENTRAL OFFICE BUDGET
(For Demonstration ONLY)

Transportation*	Budget	Pos
Director	66,568	1.0
Aides, Bus	651,677	91.0
Coordinator	127,881	3.0
Secretarial/Clerical	194,373	7.0
Bus Drivers	5,393,702	411.0
Garage Employees	781,141	24.0
Bus Service Attendant	166,383	12.0
Custodians	0	0.0
Overtime	49,000	0.0
Temporary Employees	2,300	0.0
Conf. Expenses—Admin.	500	0.0
Medical Services	13,640	0.0
Laundry/Dry Clean	6,978	0.0
Office Supplies	6,500	0.0
Vehicle Fuels	780,056	0.0
Auto/Truck Supplies	158,380	0.0
Employee Training Supplies	4,300	0.0
Trans. Vehicle Supp.	792,824	0.0
Busses, Add'l.	0	0.0
Mach/Tools, Repl.	4,410	0.0
Buses, Repl.	1,085,000	0.0
	10,285,613	549.0

*Field trip funds allocated to individual schools; otherwise, the budget has been affected little by school based management.

SAMPLE CENTRAL OFFICE BUDGET
(For Demonstration ONLY)*

Data Processing	Budget	Pos
Supervisor	61,798	1.0
Technician	334,793	9.0
Secretarial/Clerical	23,757	1.0
Overtime	2,100	0.0
Temporary Employees	0	0.0
Tuition/In-Service	0	0.0
Data Processing	0	0.0
Travel Reimbursement	428	0.0
Maintenance Service Contract	101,000	0.0
Office Supplies	51,000	0.0
Reference Materials	250	0.0
DP Equipment, Add'l.	44,115	0.0
Software, Add'l.	34,000	0.0
Equipment/Furn., Repl.	0	0.0
DP Equipment, Repl.	99,100	0.0
	752,341	11.0

*This is another example of a central office budget which does not have any of its funds allotted to the schools for school based management.

SAMPLE BUDGET PLANNING CYCLE*
(For Demonstration ONLY)

School Board approves goals and priorities for the school division	June 1
Schools develop priorities and school plans	October 1
Principals receive projected student enrollments, allocations, and budgeting materials	November 1
Schools refine school plans according to allocations and submit revised plans to central office	November 15
Superintendent reviews and approves proposed school plans	December 1
School Board reviews priorities and school plans	December 15
Principals submit proposed school budgets to central office	December 31
Proposed budgets submitted to the Superintendent	January 15
Superintendent submits proposed division budget to the School Board	March 1
School Board submits proposed budget to funding authority	April 1
Funding authority approves the division budget	April 30
Principals refine school plans according to approved budget	June 1
Principals submit budget amendments based on September 30th enrollment	October 15

*Each school system must look at its own planning and budget cycles to establish its own time lines for finalizing all budgets.

Chapter 11

The Pilot Program

Prior to converting all schools to school based management, some school systems (particularly those with many schools) may wish to experiment first with a limited number of pilot schools. Small school systems, on the other hand, may wish to develop a simulated model first, and then convert all schools. The main advantages of the pilot approach are twofold. First, the mistakes made would impact only a few schools. Second, the pilot schools allow for experimentation and learning. The result is that all schools will benefit without taking the accompanying risks or spending the extra energy involved in change.

If the pilot approach is used, here are some important guidelines:

Determine the Needed Number of Schools

Generally, districts should aim for representation from the elementary, middle, and high school levels, resulting in a minimum of three schools. In small school districts, one or two schools might be acceptable. In a school district of, say, 80,000, there might be two high schools, three middle schools, and six elementary schools, which would encompass about 10% of the student body in that situation.

Choose the Actual Schools for the Program

In choosing the actual schools, location, demographics, and willingness to participate are important considerations. To the extent possible, pilot schools should be from different geographic areas. If there are two or more pilot schools from the same level, for example the elementary level, then there should be an attempt to choose pilot elementary schools which are representative of all elementary schools in terms of size and demographics. The objective is to gain experiences in the pilot schools which are directly applicable to all other schools. This cannot be done if the pilot schools are not representative of the district as a whole. For example, it would not be wise to choose a special education school for the handicapped as a pilot school and expect the lessons learned to be applied to a regular elementary school.

The chosen schools should be from a pool of those that volunteer to participate in the pilot program. A volunteer school is not one where only the principal wants to participate, but one where there is a strong interest among parents, students, and staff to get involved. The interest level among these stakeholders can be determined by a survey developed collaboratively and issued from the principal's office.

The competency level of the principal should *not* be a factor in selecting a volunteer school unless the principal is on performance probation. It should be assumed that all principals are capable of functioning in the pilot program. If only the "best" principals were chosen, the pilot would not be a true test of workability. Strong principals can make any system work, no matter what flaws it may have. Such principals work around obstacles in order to succeed. The pilot program should determine if school based management can be carried out by *all* principals, regardless of perceived levels of competency.

Allow an Adequate Duration of Time

Remember that the conversion to school based management is not an overnight process. If the first year is spent in study and preparation, and the second and third year are devoted to the pilot project, the full conversion could be implemented at the beginning of the fourth school year. Also, coordinate conversion with the goal-setting and budget preparation cycle.

Establish Limits for the Pilot School

The pilot schools must know if there are activities they may not engage in—or even propose. For example, if the board and/or the superintendent will not allow the food service (lunch program) to be decentralized, that position should be clearly stated at the outset. If the curriculum is to be standard in all schools, then that, too, should be stipulated. Other obvious limits are:

- All laws must be obeyed.
- All federal and state regulations must be obeyed unless deviation is approved.
- All school board policies must be obeyed, unless prior approval is given.
- Administrative regulations must be followed, unless the superintendent permits otherwise.
- No contracts (for example, labor contracts) may be deviated from.
- Any accreditation standards must be met.

Other limits may be set, such as:

- The employee evaluation program shall not be changed.
- Student report cards will not be modified.
- Student transportation will be administered centrally, as in the past.
- Etcetera.

In preparing the boundaries for pilot school operation, the task force should not attempt to list *everything*. First, such a list would be endless, and second, this approach would discourage innovation. After basic limits have been set, the pilot school may *propose* anything that it wants, and do anything that is contained in their approved annual school plan. Other than that, it should be business as usual. This means that a school will follow all existing regulations and procedures, *unless it has approval to do otherwise in its school plan*. Without this rule, there is risk of losing control over the effective order of the school system, and deterioration may begin. School based management is an orderly process for improving the management of the schools, not a license for schools to do as they please. School based management has its own inevitable rules and regulations which must be followed. Teachers, principals, and other employees are "trustees" of the public interest, and all of their actions must conform with public policy.

Use a Consultant

A number of school districts have adopted various forms of decentralization, and in doing so they have done some good things and made some avoidable mistakes. A good consultant is one who is experienced and has been successful in helping other school systems decentralize. A small investment in a reputable consultant can help the pilot schools and the school system avoid unnecessary mistakes.

Fund the Pilot School the Same as Any Other School

Although the pilot schools will need a meager level of extra funding for training, visitations, consultation, and research, *the pilot schools should be given no more than their equitable share of the entire school system budget.* This is an important admonition. School based management is not a system that costs extra money to implement. Therefore, pleading requests for more money because of school based management should be rejected. It is up to the school to operate within its fair share of the school system's budget.

Establish the Format and Content of Annual School Plans

The format of annual school plans should be standardized, and this is not an unreasonable position for the superintendent to take. The superintendent is the one who must read these plans. Variations in format will only cause mistakes and confusion. The actual format of the plan, however, should be arrived at by collaboration with principals. These plans must be easy to understand and must contain a section on evaluation of the plan.

Establish the Procedure and Format for School Budgets

Most school principals have had little experience with preparing a budget that covers most of the expenses for operating the school. Therefore, an appropriate budget format and procedure needs to be tried out in the pilot program. This matter is discussed in considerable detail in Chapter Ten. It should be noted that the principals will need assistance in the form of training and support from the central office. Also, the school principal should be provided freedom within the law and administrative constraints to transfer school funds from one account to another where just cause exists.

Establish a Financial Accounting Procedure

School based management will change how funds are tracked and accounted for. The pilot program affords an excellent opportunity to discover how best to do this. Accounting procedures can be carried out most effectively with a computer program that assures both efficiency and honesty.

Include Site Committees in the Pilot Program

The use of school site committees is not optional under school based management. Every school must have such a group that meets regularly. The three main responsibilities of these committees are:

- To assist in the preparation of the annual school plan
- To assist in the preparation of the annual school budget
- To assist in improving the school in other appropriate ways

During the pilot program, the operation of these committees should be observed carefully to determine how they may be improved. If possible, the participants in these pilot committees should be given a training program.

Evaluate the Pilot Program

Without evaluation, many needed lessons will be lost. If a goal of the pilot was to develop a model which could be used in all schools, then that goal must be evaluated. If a goal was to improve scores on standardized tests for students, then test scores need to be examined and compared with non-pilot schools. If a goal was to improve the support of the pilot schools by staff, students, and parents, then some means must be devised to measure the level of support and compare that with non-pilot schools.

Obtain the Approval of the School Board Prior to Implementation

This does not mean that the board should approve every detail of the pilot plan. It does mean, however, that the board understands what the superintendent intends to do. If the superintendent has conferred regularly with the board about the project, it is unlikely that the board would stand in the way. However, the board should ask that the superintendent keep the board informed of progress and require that an evaluation of the pilot program be submitted to the board before other schools convert to school based management.

Chapter 12
Evaluation

For many school systems, school based management is a radical departure from the conventional ways of public school administration. When such a change is made, some means must be developed to gauge the impact of the change. The evaluation plan should examine not only the effects of school based management on the major mission of the school system (student learning) but also the effects of the project on school system employees, who all in some way contribute to student learning. Additionally, the evaluation must include responses from students, parents, and the community regarding the restructured management system.

Before an evaluation system can be developed, the goals of school based management must be determined through collaboration. Good possibilities for such goals are:

- To improve the quality of all instructional programs

- To provide a psychological climate which increases the effectiveness and job satisfaction of all employees

- To build a high degree of confidence in and support for the schools by parents, students, and the community

- To improve the decision-making process by allowing the staff to seek new and creative problem-solving strategies

The evaluation of school based management should focus on three kinds of data:

- Academic progress

- Attitude changes
- Impact of secondary elements

The main goal of the evaluation process is to collect highly objective data. In the area of academic progress, standardized test measures are the obvious sources of data. The measurement of attitude changes is a more difficult challenge, as results do not lend themselves to easy numerical quantification. Great care, therefore, should be taken to develop instruments that serve the needs of the school system and that provide valid and useful data.

Some of the tests which might be used to measure student academic progress are:

- Standardized norm-referenced achievement tests, such as the Iowa Test of Basic Skills
- Local school system criterion-referenced tests
- The Scholastic Aptitude Test (SAT)
- Advanced Placement Tests
- Merit Scholarship winners

A number of groups and their attitudes are affected by the implementation of school based management. Each of these groups needs to be surveyed to identify and quantify the changes in attitudes that result from their exposure to school based management. The specific groups which need to be surveyed are parents, students (grades 4-5), students (grades 6-12), teachers, classified employees (bus drivers, secretaries, etc.), and all supervisors and administrators, including principals.

School based management will influence elements other than academic progress and attitudinal changes. Although secondary in nature, these other elements are important to consider. Some secondary elements to look for are changes in:

- Student attendance
- Student suspensions and expulsions

- Staff absenteeism
- Teacher turnover
- Etcetera

Whatever secondary elements are used, evaluators must find ways to measure changes in those areas. Each local district can develop its own means of collecting data from test scores and producing its own procedures for measuring changes in secondary elements.

However, the development of a comprehensive survey procedure is complex and deserves some attention here. The following overview of the survey process is designed to give school systems some general guidelines so that they appreciate the complexity of the job, and will decide to **seek expert assistance.**

There are six major steps in surveying, and they are:

- Preparing for the survey
- Choosing the survey method
- Preparing the questionnaire
- Drawing samples
- Tabulating and analyzing returns
- Reporting results

Preparing to Survey

Before a school system decides to conduct a survey, the system should consider a number of important questions.

Why survey?

The survey is a credible, accepted means of learning how people feel about issues. Without information from parents, staff, and students regarding their views about their schools, the ability of the school board to correct problems and make improvements is seriously handicapped.

Who should be surveyed?

The major groups whose opinions should be valued and sought are students, who have the most at stake; faculty, who are responsible for teaching the students; parents, who are the taxpayers and who care greatly about how their children are treated; principals, who are central to making schools effective; classified employees, who have unique insights into how well the schools function; and supervisors and administrators, who manage every aspect of the school system.

Who should write and conduct the survey?

A special task force of representative teachers, students, parents, principals, and other administrators, assisted by an expert consultant, should oversee the plan and the entire survey process. A qualified administrator should be appointed chairperson. Unless the school system has someone on its staff who is a recognized expert in survey techniques, *no school system should prepare a survey and apply it without the direct assistance of a qualified consultant.* Without this type of help, very serious problems can arise which, in some cases, cannot be corrected.

What major activities need to be conducted?

When the task force convenes, its members should make a list of activities which need to take place and decisions which need to be made. For example, a budget for the survey needs to be developed, a consultant hired, forms prepared, a meeting schedule drawn up, etc.

What deadlines need to be established?

If a survey is to be used, it must be ready when needed. For example, if a survey is to be conducted on May 1, then a step-by-step plan must be laid out showing exactly how the survey will be made ready by that date. Many intervening deadlines must be set, such as when the first draft will be completed, when the first test survey will be completed, etc.

What is the best time to survey?

Although each school district must provide its own answer to this question, the last two weeks in May probably is the best time

Evaluation

for most school systems. The survey should take place after people have almost completed a school year, but not so late that the closing of school skews opinions or interferes with return of forms.

Choosing the Survey Method

Three common ways to conduct an opinion survey are:

- The personal interview
- The telephone interview
- The mailed questionnaire

Each of these techniques has its own unique set of advantages and disadvantages, a comparison of which is found in the next chart. At the end of this chapter is a copy of an excellent example of a survey.

SURVEY METHOD*

Method	Advantages	Disadvantages
Personal Interview	1. Higher percent of return	1. Personal and transportation costs
	2. More detailed information	2. Possibility interviewer can bias the response or record answer incorrectly
	3. Information apt to be more correct	3. Strict supervision of data collection required
	4. Misunderstandings can be cleared up by more in-depth explanation	4. Time-consuming
	5. Use of visuals possible	5. Training of interviewers required

---

* "Find Out How People Feel about Local School," National Committee for Citizens in Education, 1984, p. 16.

	6. Personal contact	6. Lack of standard approach by interviewers
		7. Volunteers needed
Telephone Interview	1. Inexpensive and fast	1. Limited to listed telephone numbers
	2. Minimal interviewer training required	2. Easy for respondent to hang up
	3. Wide geographic reach in a short time	3. Difficult to get detailed or attitudinal information
	4. Easier to call back if respondent is busy	4. Volunteers needed
	5. Small response bias because of fixed-response questions	
Mailed Questionnaire	1. Wide distribution at low cost per completed interview (mail cheaper than transportation)	1. Time-consuming; more preparation required for cover letters, follow-up and postage-paid envelopes
	2. Can reach more remote areas	2. Lower number of returns
	3. Respondents may be more honest and inclined to answer in privacy of home	3. Possibility that returns may not be representative of entire group being surveyed
	4. Shorter time in getting all surveys to respondents	4. Inability to clarify questions
	5. Fewer volunteers needed	5. Possibility that one person or group could collect many questionnaires and answer, thereby "stacking" the results
		6. Need to send reminders

Preparing the Questionnaire

Following are some practical suggestions which should help assure the quality of the questionnaire.

Never write a question alone

All survey questions should be prepared by at least two people. The stimulation and competition that exists between two participants will produce questions better than any that would be produced by only one person.

Choose question type carefully

There are only two types of questions: those that require an answer in a fixed way ("yes" or "no", for example), and those that allow an essay answer. To best receive responses regarding attitudes toward the schools, the fixed response will be used most, but there may be a need to allow for some limited essay responses as well.

Test the questionnaire for clarity and use

Before the final survey is distributed, it should be tested on a representative sample of those to be surveyed. This test will help improve the quality of the survey instrument by revealing errors and problems which the committee that prepared the survey was unable to see.

Keep the survey short

Long questionnaires will irritate some respondents, confuse others, and generally reduce the validity of the survey. Also, long questionnaires are more difficult to tabulate and analyze. The lengths of the questionnaires found at the end of this chapter are ideal.

The survey should be limited to one topic

All questions should be designed to find out how respondents feel about their schools. This major survey should avoid other topics, such as attitudes toward drugs, or sexuality education.

Where large numbers of people are being surveyed, the process should be computerized

If possible, the survey forms should be prepared so that the responses can be "bubbled" (that is, written into numbered computer forms). By doing this, all completed questionnaires can be collected and run through a scanner. Otherwise, the amount of time it takes to do the job manually can become cost-prohibitive.

Do not assume the population understands the topic being surveyed

Although officials in the school system may be knowledgeable and excited about school based management, many parents and students may know little about it. Therefore, a letter should be attached to the survey form explaining why the survey is being taken.

Delete questions to which the answers can be obtained elsewhere

Ignoring this advice simply clutters the questionnaire and causes the respondents unneeded inconvenience. For example, assuming the school system has a record of each student's birthdate, there is no reason to ask for that information on the questionnaire.

Avoid hypothetical questions

Hypothetical questions get hypothetical answers, and such answers may prove to be misleading.

The student's name should be on the surveys sent to parents

Otherwise, parents are inclined to offer opinions about schools in general, and not about their own child and their own school.

All questionnaires to different groups should share similar questions

This technique is useful in comparing the attitudes of one group with another. The questionnaire contained in this chapter includes questions that would be used for a number of different groups.

Provide space on the questionnaire for respondents to express anything they care to

Some respondents will feel that a highly structured questionnaire does not allow them to express their views fully. Providing an opportunity for parents and others to express their views on the survey forms both strengthens public relations for the school system and obtains useful information which might otherwise never be known.

Once the questionnaire is developed and put into force, it cannot be changed

The type of survey being discussed here is one that will be used permanently. Therefore, all questions must remain the same from year to year; otherwise, changes in responses from year to year cannot be measured. If the school district wishes, it can add new questions from time to time, but if these questions are to be permanent, they cannot be changed.

Individual schools should not be allowed to circulate questionnaires similar to those being circulated by the school system

Using similar questionnaires would inconvenience parents needlessly, and might cause a dispute over which responses are best or valid.

Drawing a Sample

Since the population of a survey group may be too large to survey every member (for example, parents), the survey task force may decide to survey only part of the population. At this point in the survey procedure, the assistance of an expert is needed. A number of difficult questions need to be answered. Should the sample be random? What "confidence level" is acceptable? How large should the sample be? What "skip interval" will be used? Unless there is a highly trained and experienced staff member who can properly answer these and other equally difficult questions, the task force should obtain the assistance of a qualified consultant.

Tabulating and Analyzing the Returns

After the completed questionnaires have been returned, they need to be counted to determine the proportion of those surveyed that actually responded. Then comes the difficult job of analyzing the responses to each question. Anyone can tabulate responses, but it takes an expert to analyze those responses and draw accurate conclusions. Failure to interpret the survey data correctly will give incorrect information to the public and false guidance to the school board and staff.

Reporting Results

In preparing the survey report, the following questions need to be answered.

What important points did the survey reveal?

Did the survey show an overall support for the school system? What is the attitude of respondents toward the school board? What question received the most negative response? Until the survey task force can identify all important points revealed by the survey, the report is not complete.

Are the totals significant?

Those who read the report will want to know to what extent the response level affects the accuracy of conclusions drawn from the survey.

How can questions be combined to confirm trends?

In the surveys conducted in a school system, similar questions may appear on all questionnaires, and two similar questions may appear on the same questionnaire. This would be done to confirm the reliability of certain responses. The report should explain this in terms easily understood by the average lay person.

Are results different than expected?

A survey response is always especially significant when the results are different from what was expected by the leaders of the surveying organization. This difference can mean that those in charge have been misguided in their actions.

What survey method was used?

Some persons not included in the survey (members of the press, parents not included in the survey, etc.) will want to know whether information was gathered by personal interview, telephone, or mail-out questionnaires. Whatever method was used, the report should give the rationale for using that approach.

How were the questions prepared?

The average person has a natural curiosity about how specific questions were selected, but also has little understanding or appreciation for the expertise required to select and phrase a question. An explanation of the process will help develop faith in the accuracy of the report.

Who was the sponsor of the survey?

Those not familiar with the survey, like members of the press, will want to know who authorized the survey, what did it cost, and what was the purpose.

When did the survey take place?

The report should explain why the survey was conducted during a specific period.

A copy of all of the actual questionnaires used should be included in the appendix of the report.

The following is a sample of a survey form used for parents. Similar survey forms should be developed for all administrators, teachers, non-certificated personnel, and students (grades 4 through 12). Copies of excellent survey forms for all of these groups may be obtained from the Prince William County Public Schools, Office of Staff Development, P.O. Box 389, Manassas, Virginia, 22110.

Prince William County Public Schools
1989 PARENT QUESTIONNAIRE

DIRECTIONS: Please rate the following items by placing a circle around the appropriate number representing your opinion based upon the following scale:

Excellent–1   Good–2   Fair–3   Poor–4   No Opinion–N/O

PRINCE WILLIAM COUNTY PUBLIC SCHOOL SYSTEM

The first five items relate to Prince William County Public Schools in general.

	Excellent	Good	Fair	Poor	No Opinion
1. The manner in which the Prince William County School Board reflects your point of view in its decisions.	1	2	3	4	N/O
2. The manner in which the tax dollars are spent in the school division.	1	2	3	4	N/O
3. The extent to which the school division offers appropriate instructional programs for the students.	1	2	3	4	N/O
4. The overall level of satisfaction with the performance of the School Board.	1	2	3	4	N/O
5. The overall level of satisfaction with the performance of the Superintendent.	1	2	3	4	N/O

YOUR CHILD'S SCHOOL

The remaining items focus on the school your child attends.

	Excellent	Good	Fair	Poor	No Opinion
1. The overall quality of the basic educational programs (reading, math, writing, English, science, social studies) in your child's school.	1	2	3	4	N/O
2. The level at which the educational programs are meeting your child's individual needs.	1	2	3	4	N/O
3. The level to which the educational programs are challenging your child's academic abilities.	1	2	3	4	N/O
4. Overall, the level of progress your child is making based upon your expectations.	1	2	3	4	N/O

5. Your child's motivation to learn.	1	2	3	4	N/O
6. The general instructional skills of your child's teacher(s).	1	2	3	4	N/O
7. The individualized attention your child receives from teachers.	1	2	3	4	N/O
8. The interest of the teachers toward your child.	1	2	3	4	N/O
9. The manner in which discipline is handled by the teachers in your child's school.	1	2	3	4	N/O
10. The manner in which discipline is handled by the principal/assistant principal(s) in your child's school.	1	2	3	4	N/O
11. Your feeling of your child's safety and security in school	1	2	3	4	N/O
12. The cleanliness of the school building and grounds.	1	2	3	4	N/O
13. The food served in the cafeteria at your child's school.	1	2	3	4	N/O
14. The working relationship between your child and your child's teacher(s).	1	2	3	4	N/O
15. Your overall level of satisfaction with your child's school.	1	2	3	4	N/O
16. The interest of the principal/assistant principal(s) toward your child.	1	2	3	4	N/O
17. The communication from the school staff to you.	1	2	3	4	N/O
18. Your overall level of satisfaction with the performance of the principal.	1	2	3	4	N/O
19. The extent to which you feel welcome at school.	1	2	3	4	N/O
20. Your child's enjoyment of school.	1	2	3	4	N/O

Thank you for your assistance. Please feel free to list any comments that would be beneficial to the Prince William County School Division on the bottom of this questionnaire.

Chapter 13

How to Avoid Mistakes

Under school based management, there is a significant increase in the decision-making power and the amount of money assigned to the individual school. Even though the school plan and the school budget are developed in collaboration with the site committee, and even though the principal is under the ever-watchful eyes of many parties, there is still room under the new-found independence of decentralization for making some bad mistakes. The following list has been compiled to help eliminate mistakes *before* they occur.

Understand the Phrase "Decision-Making Process" under School Based Management

The model of school based management being discussed in this book does not remove the principal from a decision-making role. Some teachers and parents would like to make binding decisions concerning the school, regardless of the principal's views. However, those who want to make decisions must remember that they are accountable for those decisions. Naturally, it would be attractive to be able to make decisions in life without accepting the consequences of those decisions, but that's not possible.

Throughout this book it has been stressed that the local school principal is held accountable for the welfare of the school. If the school is not managed properly, it is the principal (not the parents, or the teachers) who is dismissed or transferred. Nevertheless, this clear accountability placed on the principal is neither a mandate nor justification to make decisions without the involvement of stakeholders and experts. This is not to suggest that principals should seek continuous advice on routine and repetitive management trivia. Each day the typical building principal makes dozens of simple and routine decisions which require no advice from anyone.

Provide Adequate Training and Staff Development

If members of the community, school employees, and students are expected to be involved in the development of the overall plans for the operation of the school, then each of these groups needs training on such matters as group dynamics, the budgeting process, the structure of the curriculum, and similar matters of school operation. Either the central office or the local school (or a combination of the two) should provide this training.

Additionally, the local school (with assistance and advice from the central office) should maintain a continuing program of staff development for teachers and other school employees. The typical school has frequent staff turnover, making an ongoing training program for new staff members necessary. Also, changing conditions (for example, increased use of computers) requires staff development on a variety of topics.

Obtain Input from Stakeholders

If a school under school based management is to function well, it must provide opportunities for the stakeholders to be involved in many different ways. It is a serious mistake to ignore or underrepresent some faction of the school community. For example, minority parents, for a number of reasons, may be insufficiently involved in affairs of their school. The school committee and principal have a duty to reach out to all community members and bring them into the school family. If the committee is not a representative body of the entire school community, the school will soon lose touch with the needs of that community.

Avoid Overuse of Vote-Taking

In the democratic process, decisions are often made by a vote of the group. This assures that at the least the majority view is expressed, and this is as it should be in the right situation. But a majority view is not always a *representative* view. A majority vote simply reveals that the majority holds a certain position. As far as site committees are concerned, voting should be limited to a few instances where it is the only option. The trouble with voting within the advisory committee is that it creates winners and losers. The winners may be happy and get their way (for a while), but the losers may become a serious threat to united action. Rather than voting on all issues, the committee needs to arrive at a general "consensus," that is, a position which gains optimum support from the entire group. A consensus, as discussed here, does not mean that each member supports a plan 100%. A general consensus does mean, however, that all members will support the plan to some degree, or at least no member will actively work against it.

As has been mentioned, actual voting on issues should be avoided at committee meetings because such a process can divide the committee into two adversarial groups. On most issues that come before a site committee, members will have a range of views, not just "yes" or "no". For example, a committee could be trying to decide if it should devote part of its school budget for improved landscaping of the school building entrance. Discussion reveals that people have views ranging from full opposition to full support. A simple vote would force them to take either a "yes" or a "no" position, or force them to reach a position which makes no one happy. That's not the best way to determine the true position of the group.

One approach to obtain an accurate reading of the group on any issue is to use the "fist five" method. Using this tactic, a member fully in favor of the landscaping project would raise one hand with all five fingers raised, indicating complete support; however, a person totally opposed to the project would raise a fist with no fingers extended. Those with views in-between those two extreme views would express their views in the following manner:

- 5 fingers: I am for it and will work hard for it.
- 4 fingers: I am for it, will work hard and have small reservations.
- 3 fingers: For it, have serious reservations, but will go along with it.
- 2 fingers: Don't like it! Won't work for it, but will not work against it.
- 1 finger: Don't like it, won't work for it and probably will not work against it! Not sure.
- Fist: Will actively work against it—will sabotage it as it stands.

The advantage of the "fist five" approach is that it provides a clear picture of exactly where people stand. It makes reaching a consensus easier and it reduces the chance that group members will take opposing sides.

Clarify the Roles of Outside Consultants

Under school based management, a school needs to seek advice from many persons outside the school, such as curriculum specialists from the central office, business representatives, and private consultants. When such persons are brought into the school they must be briefed on their role, underscoring the *advisory* nature of their services. Similarly, the faculty should be briefed on the advisory role of all consultants used in the school. Failure to follow this rule will confuse the decision-making process. True, a competent consultant likely will suggest the best solution to a problem, but the consultant does not decide the solution. That's the function of the principal.

Place a Reserve in the School Budget

Every experienced budget-holder knows that few budget plans develop exactly according to expectations. Prices of products change and emergencies arise, making precise financial predictions unlikely. Therefore, most veteran budget-holders set aside money for unexpected events, in what is referred to as a "contingency" or "reserve" account. Most principals entering school based management for the first time have had little experience with making budgets and spending money. Therefore, at the outset of decentralization, there is the possibility of financial miscalculation. If final annual expenditures of the school are less than allowed by the budget, there is a surplus which can be applied to some planned and approved worthy cause. But, if final annual expenditures exceed that allowed by the approved budget, the principal has a problem. To avoid such mismanagement, principals need to be trained well in all matters of school budgeting. Also, the central office can help the principal avoid such problems by issuing a monthly expenditure report to each school. In this way, even if the local school is spending too much, the problem is identified early enough to correct it.

Adhere to Parameters

As previously discussed, there are countless laws, policies, regulations, contracts, etc., from which a principal may not deviate. For example, a principal may not pay teachers a salary different from that approved by the school board. Or, a principal may not stray from the requirements of a local electrical code in the installation of a new electrical outlet. In other words, there are many restrictions on a principal's freedom to act independently. A principal who strays beyond these limits without prior approval in the school plan can face serious consequences. For example, one principal decided to deviate from the pay scale for extra duties (coaching, etc.) without the prior approval of the school board. Although the actions of the principal were well-intentioned and honest, and the problem easy to correct, such unauthorized actions and similar violations could create serious mismanagement. Under school based management, all principals should observe this guideline: *"Principals can do anything they wish, if their actions are approved in the school plan; otherwise, it's business as usual."*

Keep Parents Informed

It is not enough to simply organize a good site committee which is properly representative of the community. A principal (with the advice of the school committee) must also devise ways to ensure that the entire school community is kept informed of school affairs generally. For example, a committee might be preparing the school plan, but if the community is unaware of this fact, there is likely to be little opportunity for suggestions from the community. Or, the school might be in the process of changing the student report card format and procedure. In this case, the school should alert the parents of the coming change. It is the principal's job to keep parents informed of the important things that occur regularly at the school. Failure to do so can result in a communications breakdown and a waste of limited energies.

Stay In Charge

Functioning well as a school principal under school based management requires a host of special skills and attitudes. The principal must learn to walk a narrow and winding path between participatory and autocratic management. Most school districts have faced the experience of a principal who "lost control" of the school, or a principal who tried to run the school as a dictatorship. Neither extreme is acceptable. The successful school based management principal must learn how to get the best advice and effort from school employees, students, and parents, and how to make the right decisions at the right time.

Understand the Role of the Central Office

Even under the centralized mode of school operation, it is often difficult to achieve mutual understanding of the roles of the central office and the local school. Under the centralized approach to administration, the central office gives a great deal of direction in matters pertaining to the operation of the individual school. Under this system, the local principal is a kind of "conduit" for decisions made by higher authority. Under decentralized management, the local school principal is required to make more independent decisions without direction from the central office. But even under localized school management, the central office continues to carry on many important functions. Again, the principal must remember that all business continues to be practiced according to the *status quo*, unless the principal has approval to act otherwise. Failure to understand and practice this concept can create unnecessary error and confusion.

Apply Discretionary Powers Carefully

It is true that the "power" of the principal increases under school based management, but the principal must be careful not to misunderstand and misapply this new-found power. In one case a principal established a "special supplies" account, which the advisory committee and the central office believed to be a fund for meeting unexpected school supply needs. After several months, a pattern appeared in the use of this fund. Little by little, possibly to avoid attention, the principal bought items one by one, which when taken in total would have resulted in a lavishly decorated office for the principal. All principals need an office equipped for efficiency, and there is nothing wrong with an office that is maintained in an attractive manner. One can even argue that there is nothing wrong with a lavishly furnished office, *if* that's how the community wants to spend its limited funds. But in this case, there was no clear understanding, except by the principal, of how the "special supplies" account was to be used. As a result, the principal was placed on probation, and faced a serious handicap in future working relations with the community.

Keep Student Learning as the Highest Priority

The inherent problem in the anecdote related above was the principal's failure to view the school's priorities properly. The major purpose of the schools is to assure that students learn certain approved skills and knowledge and practice acceptable behavior. Although a lavishly decorated principal's office might contribute indirectly to such purposes, there are other expenditures which likely would be more effective in improving student learning and behavior. When the local school plan is being prepared, the learning welfare of the students must be kept foremost in mind. A school site committee may want to beautify a school by spending money on landscape improvements, but the question which should be asked before making such a decision is: "Will school landscape improvements contribute more to improved student learning than some other project would?" Failure to place student learning as the highest priority can result in not getting the full benefit of each limited tax dollar.

Be Open-Minded

Sometimes a principal becomes so egotistical that the principal ignores the good advice and assistance of others. All principals should be ambitious to serve the best interests of the school system generally and the local school specifically. However, an overly ambitious principal can become overly self-centered and view everything in terms of self-interest. We all know people who are obsessed with getting attention, who are driven to prove how intelligent or successful they are. Such people have stepped over the line of acceptable behavior. A principal will receive all of the attention needed just by seeking soliciting and using good advice and by concentrating on the needs of students.

Use Delegation Properly

No principal can operate a school alone. A principal cannot teach all the students, clean the building, and complete all the needed paperwork. That's why principals have teachers, custodians, and secretaries. No matter how small a school is, a principal must arrange through delegation the work of employees and community volunteers to produce the best, most productive school possible. Delegation means directing others to carry out certain responsibilities. Knowing how to delegate effectively is based upon a combination of experience, study, analysis, and intuition. Failure to delegate not only stifles the use of available help, but it creates a "bottleneck" in the principal's office. Those who can't delegate often are unable to "let go" and end up trying to do everything themselves. As a result, the good efforts of others often lay on the principal's desk. Under school based management, the principal who wants to do everything himself is doomed to failure.

Be Willing to Take Risks

The whole purpose in decentralizing the school system's organization is to allow the individual schools to find better, more effective, and more efficient ways to provide for the learning of students. The principal is expected to show some imagination in the management of the school and to encourage and support others in seeking better ways of operating the school. During the first few years under school based management, not all principals will develop new and creative approaches. The concept of local management is new to most principals, and it takes time to learn to use it creatively. Some principals are inclined to let others do the pioneer work first. Others will not be convinced that school based management is a permanent development until it has become the official way of doing things. But eventually, all principals must accept the spirit of decentralization, challenge old ways of operating, and try new ways. If a school continues unchanged under school based management, the first place to look is in the principal's office.

The suggestions in this chapter may help school principals and other administrators avoid the mistakes which can be made as a result of the change to school based management.

Chapter 14

DOs & DON'Ts

The following information is for those who are thinking about converting to school based management, and is designed as a quick summary of recommended actions and actions to be avoided. Many of the points here are discussed in greater detail elsewhere in this book.

- ✓ **DO be committed.** To the extent that staff, parents, the superintendent and the school board are not committed, then to that extent the success of school based management will be hindered.

- ✗ **DON'T allow undermining.** Once a decision by general agreement has been reached to enter into school based management, and once the board has adopted a policy supporting decentralization and the superintendent has laid out directions (as the result of collaboration), actions contrary to this position should not be acceptable and should be corrected through proper supervision.

- ✓ **DO your homework.** There is much written about the decentralization of management, seminars are regularly available, successful models can be visited, and expert, experienced consultants are available.

- ✗ **DON'T move without adequate information.** There is no excuse for entering into school based management before a school system is ready. By taking enough time and investing a little extra energy, a school district should be able to avoid the many mistakes made by others.

✓ **DO set up a pilot—real or simulated.** In school districts where there are numerous schools, it may be advisable to try school based management on a pilot basis, using at least one school from each level. In other instances, planners can create a model by simulation, especially if computers are available.

✗ **DON'T jump into the unknown.** The purpose of a pilot is to learn about a new approach and to limit damage when an error is made. Once a pilot has operated successfully, there is better hope of success for all schools.

✓ **DO establish parameters.** Before individual schools begin to develop their local school plans, they are entitled to know what the limits are. Otherwise, the plans will contain proposals which are not acceptable or even subject to consideration.

✗ **DON'T overdo it, however.** Although the parameters should prohibit actions which are clearly unacceptable, the parameters should be sufficiently broad so that innovative and potentially worthwhile proposals can be given serious consideration.

✓ **DO put new staff roles in writing.** The decentralization of management changes the description of many employment positions. Therefore, every job description should be examined for needed changes. Approved revisions should be published for all to see.

✗ **DON'T allow uncertainty about roles.** Successful school based management requires a strong dose of coordination, which is hampered by the lack of clear job descriptions and organizational charts.

✓ **DO transfer all appropriate funds to the schools.** There is a direct correlation between the amount of money transferred to the schools and the school system's commitment to school based management.

✗ **DON'T hold back or hide funds.** To do so would undermine the credibility of the central office in the eyes of those in the school and community. The formula for allocating funds should be developed collaboratively and should be available for public review. Otherwise, those in the school will suspect that the central office is not being faithful to the principles of decentralization.

✓ **DO transfer corresponding decision-making power along with funds.** If the schools are allocated funds to purchase instructional supplies, then the local school should have the authority to decide what supplies are needed. This advice, however, should not be interpreted to mean that a local school can buy *anything* it wants in the name of instructional supplies. Naturally, there are certain legal restraints on purchases and certain reasonable guidelines which must be followed.

✗ **DON'T be afraid to let go.** Within applicable legal requirements and reasonable regulations, the local schools can make intelligent spending choices. Therefore, schools should be allowed reasonable discretion in how they spend their money.

✓ **DO develop an equitable distribution of funds.** One recommended approach to allocating funds is described in Chapter Ten. Whatever approach the school system uses, it should assure educational equity. And, "equity" does not necessarily mean "equal". Equity here means the distribution of funds to the schools based on principles of fairness and justice.

✗ **DON'T develop this funding formula in private.** The decision on how to distribute funds to the schools should be arrived at by a special task force which represents the various interests of the school system. The meetings of this task force should be open and its minutes should be made available. The final task force report should be presented at an open public meeting before it is finally and officially submitted to the superintendent. Hopefully, the final outcome is a procedure to which everyone generally agrees and one which is generally understood. Anything less runs the risk of being undermined by doubts and suspicion. It is very important that the distribution procedure be fair (equitable) and that those in the central office, on the school board, and those in the schools believe in the fairness of the procedure.

✓ **DO transfer funds in a lump sum.** The ideal way to allocate funds to the schools is on a "lump-sum" basis. This means that each school receives one grant of funds which may be spent generally as the school wishes (according to an approved plan and budget).

✗ **DON'T piecemeal the transfer of funds.** Some school districts transfer funds to the schools in *categories*. This means that allocated funds must be spent according to a decision made elsewhere. For example, money transferred to a school in the category "field trips" could only be spent for field trips. Under a lump-sum allocation, there is no such centrally-imposed restriction on how the money will be spent. Complete school based management suggests that the individual school has great leeway in using its funds. The best way to accomplish this is through the use of lump-sum allocations and highly flexible money transfers within the local school budget.

✓ **DO spend money in the best interests of student education.** All goals of the school system and the individual schools should be rooted in the educational welfare of students. Therefore, all school budgets should be examined by the superintendent to assure that the largest share of funds go to this purpose. All school plans must show how spending is expected to improve the school's educational program.

✗ **DON'T spend money just for the sake of administrative convenience.** A proposal to redecorate the principal's office, or a proposal to purchase a car phone for the principal, should be looked at initially with considerable skepticism. Each school plan needs to be reviewed carefully, since some principals may tend to use their influence for improving personal convenience and comfort.

✓ **DO develop creative school plans.** School based management causes schools to be different. School based management allows schools to solve problems that could not be solved previously. School based management encourages innovation and creativity. Therefore, annual school plans and budgets should reflect this.

✗ **DON'T submit conventional plans.** Although it is difficult for some schools to change their long-standing ways of doing things, a superintendent should be skeptical of any school plan that is no different than previous plans used when schools were administered centrally. Schools are different; therefore, their plans should be different. Schools have complex problems; therefore, plans should contain innovative solutions to those problems.

✓ **DO develop a proper budget for the school plan.** A budget is a numerical expression of a written school plan. The school plan is a written expression of the numerical school budget. The two must complement and supplement each other. Although the local school budget is not a fixed document (the school should be allowed to make mid-stream adjustments), it should express clearly in dollars exactly how the school plans to spend its money during the coming school year.

✗ **DON'T get careless with the school budget.** Budgets are supposed to be the best expression possible of how money is intended to be spent over a given period of time. Although transfers from one school account to another should be allowed, they should be for good cause and with prior permission. For example, if a principal indicates that $5,000 will be spent on computers but actually spends that amount for carpeting, that would be an unacceptable deviation without explanation or prior approval of the principal's supervisor.

✓ **DO take the lead.** Although a site committee should be required in all schools, and although this committee should have a very close, collaborative relationship with the principal, it is the responsibility of the principal to take the leadership role in making good things happen in the school.

✗ **DON'T dominate.** Some view an effective principal to be one who gets his way by any possible means. This kind of leader may practice deception, disinformation, manipulation, and intimidation to achieve objectives. These are not the tactics of an effective principal under school based management. An effective principal is one who can lead a group to consensus and one who can bring out the best in each group member. An effective principal is one who can, when needed, set aside personal desires in the interest of the will of the committee. This does not mean that principals should never say "no" to a committee. In some instances, principals must, in good conscience, veto the committee's position.

However, if the committee is properly selected (or, elected), the principal will receive good advice and will seldom need to say "no".

✓ **DO collaborate among stakeholders.** Parents, students, staff, and the principal should all work together in an attempt to achieve agreement on the best interests of the school. No one group within the committee (e.g., parents) should attempt to force their special interest on others. The educational welfare of students should override most special interests of the committee.

✗ **DON'T make decisions by command.** Under school based management, each school should have reasonable discretion to meet the educational needs of its community. The central office should stay out of discretionary affairs, and restrict its own direction to other areas. At the school level, neither the principal nor any special interest group should dominate the school family. The principal, the union, the staff, the parents, and the students should focus their attention on the educational program and try to make their decisions through consensus-building.

✓ **DO provide training.** Parents, staff, and students need to be trained in consensus-building, conflict resolution, and team leadership. Principals need training in leading by collaboration and in developing and managing school budgets. The school board needs to develop a thorough understanding of how school based management works.

✗ **DON'T skimp on this task.** Management decentralization changes the role of all parties in various ways. Without adequate training, "business as usual" will prevail. The failure to provide a thorough staff development program can interfere seriously with success.

✓ **DO have the superintendent approve plans.** School based management should allow schools to be different; however, school based management is not a license for schools to do anything they wish. The schools are public property and are run by trustees of the public's best interest. They must operate within policy, and all actions taken by all employees must be within those policies. Therefore, *somebody* must approve plans which tell how the schools will be operated. This responsibility is clearly an executive function belonging to the superintendent.

✗ **DON'T have the school board approve the plans.** The superintendent should give the board copies of school plans and the board should study them, ask questions, and offer suggestions. However, the board should not formally approve the plans, since that puts the board into the administration of the schools. Also, by officially approving the plans, the board makes schools less accountable. In various ways, the board can continue to exercise reasonable control over the school system without actually approving every school plan every year.

✓ **DO assign accountability clearly.** When job descriptions are rewritten, each one should have a clear accountability statement. In this way incumbents know what is expected of them and what to expect from others.

✗ **DON'T leave any doubt regarding accountability.** Not only should all employees know their responsibilities, but each school should be held accountable for its actions. Naturally, this focuses attention on the principal, but it also makes other school staff members more accountable.

✓ **DO set up a means by which to evaluate school based management.** There are various ways to accomplish this. As discussed in this book, an annual survey of parents, students, and staff is very effective. Also, the annual collection of student standardized test data can be useful. In any case, there must be an effective means by which to discover what is being done right and what is being done wrong.

✗ **DON'T wait.** No recommendation for school based management is complete without a procedure for evaluating progress. Therefore, decentralization should not begin until this matter has been finalized.

✓ **DO look for results.** If there is no agreement on what results are expected from the schools, there is a temptation to focus on methodology and play down results. Sometimes schools adopt supposedly reliable methods, assuming that they guarantee results, but too often the intended results are not clear, or no real attempt is made to actually measure those results.

✗ **DON'T dwell on methodology.** Although the superintendent (or his designee) should be interested in the various methodologies being followed in the schools, there should be more interest directed at results. Furthermore, in approving school plans, the principal's supervisor should be reluctant to approve methods to be used but quick to approve final results. If the supervisor approves certain methods to be used, the principal's accountability declines. It is difficult for the supervisor to criticize the principal for any failures, because the supervisor approved the methods used. For example, a supervisor should approve a goal to increase reading levels by a specific amount, but should not approve the methods aimed at achieving that goal.

✓ **DO keep the school board informed.** One of the worst mistakes the superintendent can make is to allow a situation to develop in which the school board must use the local newspaper to find out what is happening in the schools. It is the superintendent's critical responsibility to keep the board informed of significant activities in the schools, and failure to do so is a serious mistake.

✗ **DON'T ignore questions and objections of the school board.** Not only must the superintendent keep the board informed, he or she must be willing to answer questions and respond to any concerns which board members may have. Although the superintendent should not allow the board to usurp executive responsibilities, the superintendent should listen intently and weigh seriously any suggestions or concerns the board may have.

✓ **DO deal fairly with the union.** Unions and the employees they represent have specific legal rights and protections under various labor relations statutes. These provisions must be obeyed until changed by agreement, or until the law is changed. But if the union wants fair consideration for its concerns, it should give equally fair consideration to the needs of school based management.

✗ **DON'T attempt to deceive the union.** Trust and respect are two important ingredients in the success of any organization. If the union is not kept informed of issues important to it, and if union opinion is not sought with regard to labor relations issues, the credibility of management will be reduced. By the same token, the union should show similar respect for the needs of management to keep education as its uppermost priority.

✓ **DO be patient with conversion.** The shift from a highly centralized form of administration to a highly decentralized one is time consuming (particularly in larger school systems) because of the many changes required and resulting uneasiness among staff. Change must come at its own pace; that is, only as the leading players are willing to move.

✗ **DON'T rush.** In one school district the substantive conversion to decentralized management took place in three years from the day the superintendent asked the staff to explore a more decentralized structure of management. The first year was spent in studying various approaches, the building of a simulated structure, and the selection and preparation of five pilot schools. The second and third years were devoted to the pilot program and preparation for system-wide conversion at the end of the third year. This was break-neck speed for a large school system, and should not be seen as routine. Whatever length of time it takes to do it right is the time that must be taken.

✓ **DO be willing to take chances.** Principals who are effective at taking calculated risks have an advantage over less adventurous people in terms of school based management. The discretionary funds and powers given to a school provide the basic ingredients for bringing about innovative change. All that is needed to complete the recipe are a few shakers and movers who are willing to try something new. It is helpful if the principal is one such person.

✗ **DON'T continue business as usual.** One of the barriers to decentralization is the *status quo*. This existing state of affairs is the result of conflicting forces which find a balance. To change the *status quo*, other overpowering forces of change must emerge. This is a tall order for the public schools, since they are now entrenched in politics, tradition, and law—powerful forces to overcome. But the changed management should create a new setting for the individual school, allowing for a challenge of the *status quo* and a fresh approach to old problems.

✓ DO try to achieve consensus. The purpose of the site committee is to lead the school by consensus toward improved education. The strength of the decisions made by the committee is primarily due to the fact that its decisions garner the most support of all stakeholders.

✗ DON'T vote on site committee decisions. When members of a group vote on an issue, there can be two problems. First, a vote is generally two-sided; that is, one must respond to an issue as "for" or "against", allowing for no compromises inbetween. So votes can be an inaccurate way of discovering voters' views. Second, when committee members vote, there are winners and losers—and losers have long memories. In other words, voting by "yes" or "no" blocks cooperation by the group. Therefore, other methods of discovering members' views need to be used. One such approach, which is very effective, is discussed elsewhere in this book.

✓ DO stay within the budget. A school budget is the principal's best plan for how to spend money during the next school year. The school should abide by its budget unless there are unforeseen and uncontrollable circumstances that force officials to reconsider. If such circumstances arise and provide good reason for change, the principal should be allowed to transfer funds from one account to another.

✗ DON'T overrun the budget. One of the most serious mistakes a principal can make under school based management is to spend beyond the limits approved for the total school budget. Unless convincing excuses exist, this should be viewed as mismanagement by higher authority, subject to swift and decisive corrective action. However, such errors should be infrequent if principals have been provided with training and supervision.

✓ **DO organize site committees on a representative basis.** Some principals try to direct the makeup of site committees, and that's often a mistake, especially when the principal is caught. The site committee should be composed of people who are representative of the various groups in the school zone—parents, community, students, and staff. It is usually wise to select such people by voting.

✗ **DON'T leave out key interests.** Each school needs to look at its demographics and decide what makes up a "representative" group and how representatives of such groups should be chosen. Some groups (minorities, for example) are sometimes reluctant to become involved. In such cases, a special "reach-out" effort may be called for. The National Committee for Citizens in Education (Columbia, MD) offers an excellent training program in getting disenfranchised groups active in school affairs.

✓ **DO stay within parameters.** No school system should enter into school based management without an understood set of guidelines. A principal can expect correction from above if the school becomes involved in activities which are outside of or contrary to board policy or school based management guidelines.

✗ **DON'T go out on a limb.** For example, a school system might prohibit school-sponsored travel to foreign countries when school is in session. This same school system, however, might also allow schools to exercise discretion in matters of field trips. In such a case, the principal would be well advised to seek permission before approving a field trip abroad.

Appendix

Do You Have School Based Management?

The following survey is used by the author as an initial attempt to determine to what extent a school system is practicing the principles, strategies and tactics of school based management.

1. What portion of the total school system operating budget is allocated to the schools?
2. Are these allocations equitable (e.g., student based)?
3. Are the school allocations "lump-sum"?
4. Does the school board have a policy authorizing school based management?
5. Does the superintendent actively support school based management?
6. Does the school board support school based management?
7. Is there a significant conflict between the union and management over school based management?
8. How much discretion do schools have to expend funds allocated to them?
9. Is the payment of utilities school based?
10. To what extent are maintenance costs school based?

11. How many bosses does a principal have?

12. How many layers of bureaucracy are there between the principal and the superintendent?

13. Are central office positions "directive" or "consultive"?

14. Is there a local site committee at each school representative of staff, parents (community), and students?

15. How is the chairperson selected?

16. Does the committee have a major role in the preparation of the annual school plan and annual school budget?

17. Does the committee meet regularly?

18. Does the committee have a real influence in the nature of the school?

19. Has there been a training program for everybody?

20. Does the school system operate under goals which have been developed by all parties-in-interest?

21. Are these goals actively sought?

22. Is the local school held accountable for its success or failure?

23. Is there an evaluation procedure based upon accountability?

24. Is the evaluation procedure based more on the measurement of results than an analysis of methodology?

25. Do students have a choice of which school to attend?

26. Are the school different? In what ways?

27. What powers reside in the central office?

28. What powers reside within the school?

29. Is there high satisfaction among customers?

30. Are there acrimonious disputes at the board level over school based management issues?

31. Is there a good financial accounting system for each school?

32. Do local school "stakeholders" have a common understanding of the goals of their school?

33. Are decisions made more by collaboration or more by authority and/or coercion? Do all parties share this view?

34. Can the individual school determine the number and configuration of personnel?

35. To what extent are different creative activities taking place in the schools?

36. Is there a healthy competition among schools?

37. Who officially approves school plans?

38. Are those affected by decisions given a significant voice in making those decisions?

39. What are the official parameters for school based management?

40. How are conflicts resolved between principals (schools) and the central office?

41. Can schools carry over funds from year to year?

42. How detailed are school board policies and administrative regulations?

43. How do local site committees make decisions?

44. What is the superintendent's style for making decisions?

45. To what extent does the instructional program vary from school to school?

46. Does the superintendent meet regularly with representatives of school staffs, parents, and students?

47. What happens when a school fails?

48. What happens when a school succeeds?

Bibliography

BOOKS

An ACCESS Printout on School Based Improvement and Effective Schools: A Perfect Match for Bottom-Up Reform. Columbia, MD: National Committee for Citizens in Education, 1988.

Avery, Michel, et. al. *Building United Judgment: A Handbook for Consensus Decision Making.* Madison, WI: The Center for Conflict Resolution, 1981.

Beck, Arthur C., and Ellis D. Hillmar. *Positive Management Practices: Bringing Out the Best in Organizations and People.* San Francisco: Jossey-Bass, 1987.

Blake, Robert R., et. al. *Spectacular Teamwork: How to Develop the Leadership Skills for Team Success.* U.S.A., 1987.

Buchholz, Steve, and Thomas Roth. *Creating the High Performance Team.* U.S.A.: Wilson Learning Corp., 1987.

Francis, Dave, and Don Young. *Improving Work Groups: A Practical Manual for Team Building.* San Diego: University Associates, 1979.

Greenhalgh, John. *School Site Budgeting: Decentralized School Management.* Lanham, MD: University Press of America, 1984.

Henderson, Anne T., Carl L. Marburger, and Theodora Ooms. *Beyond the Bake Sale: An Educator's Guide to Working With Parents.* Columbia, MD: National Committee for Citizens in Education, 1986.

Lawler III, Edward E. *High-Involvement Management: Participative Strategies for Improving Organizational Performance.* San Francisco: Jossey-Bass, 1986.

Lewis, James, Jr. *Achieving Excellence in Our Schools: by Taking Lessons from America's Best-Run Companies.* Westbury, N.Y.: J.L. Wilkerson, 1986.

Lewis, James, Jr. *Creating Excellence in Our Schools: by Taking More Lessons from America's Best-Run Companies.* Westbury, N.Y.: J.L. Wilkerson, 1986.

Lewis, James, Jr. *Re-creating Our Schools for the 21st Century: Managing America's Schools with Distinction.* Westbury, N.Y.: J.L. Wilkerson, 1987.

Maeroff, Gene I. *The Empowerment of Teachers: Overcoming the Crisis of Confidence.* New York: Teachers College Press, 1988.

Marburger, Carl L. *One School at a Time: School Based Management: A Process for Change.* Columbia, MD: National Committee for Citizens in Education, 1985.

NASSP Bulletin. Reston, VA: National Association of Secondary School Principals, September 1989.

Peters, Tom, and Nancy Austin. *A Passion for Excellence: The Leadership Difference.* New York: Random House, 1985.

Peters, Tom. *Thriving on Chaos: Handbook for a Management Revolution.* New York: Knopf, 1987.

Pierce, Lawrence C. *School Site Management.* Cambridge, MA: Aspen Institute for Humanistic Studies, 1977.

Reddy, W. Brendan. *Team Building: Blueprints for Productivity and Satisfaction.* Alexandria, VA: NTL Institute for Applied Behavioral Science, 1988.

Rosaler, Jean. *How to Make the Best School Site Council in the World: A Guidebook for School Improvement Councils and Other Community Groups.* Sacramento: California State Department of Education, 1979.

Rosow, Jerome M., and Robert Zager. *Allies in Educational Reform: How Teachers, Unions, and Administrators Can Join Forces for Better Schools.* San Francisco: Jossey-Bass, 1989.

School-Based Management: Communication Workshop Kit. Arlington, VA: National School Public Relations Association, 1989.

Waterman, Robert H. *The Renewal Factor: How the Best Get and Keep the Competitive Edge.* New York: Bantam Books, 1987.

White, Paula A. *Resource Materials on School-Based Management.* New Brunswick, NJ: Center for Policy Research in Education, 1988.

PERIODICALS

"American Federation of Teachers Talks Revolution." *American School Board Journal,* October 1989.

"Annual School-Based Plan Budget. 1988-89 Planning and Budgeting for Educational Management." Duval County Schools, Jacksonville, FL, 1988, 20 pages.

Beers, Donald E. "School Based Management." Charleston (SC) County School District, 1984, 19 pages.

Blackburn, Harold. "How To Locate Leadership: Put Down Your Buckets!" *National Association of Secondary School Principals Bulletin* April 1984.

Burns, Leonard T., and Jeanne Howes. "Handing Control to Local Schools: Site-Based Management Sweeps the Country." *The School Administrator* August 1988: 8-10.

Burton, Nancy, et. al. "School-Based Planning Manual. Part I: A Step-by-Step Planning Guide." Seattle Public Schools, Washington Department of Planning, Research and Evaluation, January 1982.

Caldwell, Brian J. "Educational Reform Through School-Site Management: An International Perspective on the Decentralization of Budgeting." Conference of the American Education Finance Association. Arlington, VA, March 26-28, 1987.

Caldwell, Brian J. "Resource Allocation at the School Level: An Examination of School-Based Budgeting in Canada and the United States." National Conference on Educational Administration of the Australian Council for Educational Administration. August 31-September 5, 1980.

Carr, Rex A. "Second-Wave Reforms Crest at Local Initiative." *The School Administrator* August 1988: 16-18.

Casner-Lotto, Jill. "Expanding the Teacher's Role: Hammond's School Improvement." *Phi Delta Kappan* January 1988: 349-353.

Cawelti, Gordon. "Key Elements of Site-Based Management." *Educational Leadership* May 1989: 46.

Clinchy, Evans. "Public School Choice: Absolutely Necessary but Not Wholly Sufficient." *Phi Delta Kappan* December 1989: 289-294.

Conley, Sharon C., Timothy Schmidle, and Joseph B. Shedd. "Teacher Participation in the Management of School Systems." *Teachers College Record* 90.2 (1988).

Cooper, Bruce S., et. al. "Incentives That Work: An Administrative Innovation in the Dade County Schools." *Phi Delta Kappan* April 1980: 523-524.

David, Jane L., and Susan M. Peterson. "Can Schools Improve Themselves? A Study of School-Based Improvement Programs." Palo Alto, CA: Bay Area Research Group, 1984.

David, Jane L. "Synthesis of Research on School-Based Management," *Educational Leadership* May 1989: 45-53.

Davidson, Jack L., and Margaret A. Montgomery. "Instructional Leadership System Research Report." Tyler (TX) Independent School District, March 1985, 50 pages.

"Decentralized Decision-Making." *Educational Research Service Information Aid* March 1975.

Dreyfuss, Gerald. "Dade County Opens Doors to Site Decisions." *The School Administrator* August 1988: 12-15.

Finn, Chester E., Jr. "Education That Works: Make the Schools Complete." *Harvard Business Review* September-October 1987.

Finn, Chester E., Jr. "Toward Strategic Independence: Nine Commandments for Enhancing School Effectiveness." *Phi Delta Kappan* April 1984: 518-524.

Geisert, Gene. "The New Union Juggernaut is Disguised As a Bandwagon." *The Executive Educator* August 1989.

Genck, Fredric H. "How to Improve Performance Results in Your District." *School Administrator* August 1987: 17-19.

Glenn, Charles L. "Putting School Choice in Place." *Phi Delta Kappan* December 1989: 295-300.

Gomez, Joseph J. "The Path to School-Based Management Isn't Smooth, But We're Scaling the Obstacles One By One." *The American School Board Journal* October 1989.

Gonder, Peggy Odell "Anatomy of a School Success." *The Executive Educator* January 1983.

Guthrie, James W. "School-Based Management: The Next Needed Education Reform." *Phi Delta Kappan* December 1986: 305-309.

Hall, Susan Hlesciak. "Can School-Centered Child Care Programs End Parents' Worry Over Latchkey Children?" *Network* 14.4 (1989).

Hanuskek, Eric A. "The Impact of Differential Expenditures on School Performance." *Educational Researcher* May 1989: 45-51, 62.

Harris, George W. "Managing Your Warehousing System." *School Business Affairs* February 1987: 20-23.

Harrison, Cynthia R. "Site-Based Management: The Realities of Implementation." *Educational Leadership* May 1989: 55-58.

Heddinger, Fred M. "Do Your School Principals Have Enough Decision-Making Power?" *The American School Board Journal* February 1978.

Heller, Robert W., et. al. "You Like School-Based Power, but You Wonder if Others Do." *Executive Educator* November 1989.

Herman, Jerry J. "A Decision-Making Model: Site-Based Communications/Governance Committees," *NASSP Bulletin* December 1989: 61-66.

Honeyman, David S., and Rich Jensen. "School-Site Budgeting." *School Business Affairs* February 1988: 12-14.

"Increased School Site Management: Implications for Central Support (Consultant) Services." Edmonton Public Schools, Edmonton, Alberta, Canada, 11 pages.

Kearns, David T. "Let the Free Market Reign." *The School Administrator* April 1990.

Keene, T. Wayne. "School-Based Management: Missing Link in Accountability?" *Education* 101.1 (1980).

Kennelly, Catherine A. "Converting to School-by-School Budgeting" *School Business Affairs* October 1984: 44-45.

Kirst, Michael W. "Who Should Control Our Schools." *Education Policy* January 1988: 74-79.

Lagana, Joseph F. "Ready, Set, Empower! Superintendents Can Sow the Seeds for Growth." *The School Administrator* January 1989: 20-22.

Lindelow, John. "School-Based Management." *School Leadership: Handbook for Survival*. Alexandria, VA: ERIC, 1981.

Lezotto, Lawrence W. "School Effectiveness: Reflections and Future Directions." Annual Meeting of the American Educational Research Association. San Francisco, April 16-20, 1986.

MacKenzie, Donald, and Ted Urich. "Support Staff Workshops—A Method to Develop PR Skills and Improve Productivity." *NASSP Bulletin* April 1984: 137-139.

McConaghy, Tom. "The Quiet Revolution: School-Based Budgeting." *Phi Delta Kappan* February 1989: 486-487.

Neal, Richard G. "School-Based Management Lets Principals Slice the Budget Pie." *The Executive Educator* January 1989.

Parker, Barbara. "School Based Management: Improve Education by Giving Parents, Principals More Control of Your School." *The American School Board Journal* July 1979.

Payzant, Thomas W. "To Restructure Schools, We've Changed the Way the Bureaucracy Works." *American School Board Journal* October 1989.

Pearson, Judith. "A Response to Joe Nathan." *Phi Delta Kappan* December 1989: 308-310.

Pierce, Lawrence C. "School Based Management." Eugene, OR: Oregon School Study Council, 1980.

Prasch, John C. "Reversing the Trend Toward Centralization." *Educational Leadership* October 1984: 27-29.

Rist, Marilee C. "Here's What Empowerment Will Mean for Your School." *The Executive Educator* August 1989.

"School-Site Management." *The Practitioner* December 1989: 1-6.

"School-Site Management—In Britain." Minneapolis: Humphrey Institute.

Shanker, Albert. "Does Money Make A Difference?" *The New York Times* May 1989.

Sirotnik, Kenneth A. "The School as the Center of Change." Brackenridge Forum for the Enhancement of Teaching. San Antonio, TX, August 18-21, 1987.

"Site-Managed Schools." *Organizing for Learning: Toward the 21st Century*. Reston, VA: National Association of Secondary School Principals, 1989, pp. 16-20.

Smilanich, Bob. "Devolution in Edmonton Public Schools: Ten Years Later." Edmonton Public Schools, Alberta, Canada, 14 pages.

Spear, JoAnn Palmer. "School Site Budgeting/Management: The State of the Art." Annual Meeting of the American Educational Research Association. Montreal, Canada, April 11-15, 1983.

Steller, Arthur W. "Effective Schools Research: Practice and Promise." Phi Delta Kappa Fastback 276, 1988.

St. John, Donna. "A Unique Labor-Management Partnership Has Made Dade County Public Schools a Model in Education Reform." U.S. Department of Labor: Labor-Management Brief Number 16, 1989.

Stewart, G. Kent. "Some Old Questions Revisited." *CEFP Journal* September-October 1985: 12-14.

Timar, Thomas. "The Politics of School Restructuring." *Phi Delta Kappan* December 1989: 265-275.

Uchitelle, Susan. "What It Really Takes to Make School Choice Work." *Phi Delta Kappan* December 1989: 301-303.

Weischadle, David E. "School-Based Management and the Principal." *Clearing House* October 1980: 53-55.

Welsh, Patrick. "Are Administrators Ready to Share Decision Making with Teachers?" *American Educator* Spring 1987: 23, 25, 47-48.

Woodworth, Beth E. "Barriers Block the Path to School-Based Power." *The Executive Educator* November 1989: 17.

CASSETTE TAPES

Bienstock, Eric M. "Creative Problem Solving." Warner Communications Co.

Blanchard, Kenneth and Spencer Johnson. "One Minute Manager." Random House, 1987.

Cocco, Susan. "Assertiveness Training." Random House, 1988.

Nierenberg, Gerard I. "The Art of Negotiation." Random House, 1987.

DO YOU HAVE AN IDEA TO SHARE?

The National Educational Service is always looking for high-quality manuscripts that have practical application for educators and others who work with youth.

Do you have a new, innovative, or especially effective approach to some timely issue? Does one of your colleagues have something burning to say on curriculum development, professionalism in education, excellence in teaching, or some other aspect of education? If so, let us know. We'd like to hear from you. Tell us that reading Richard Neal's book gave you an incentive to contact us.

Nancy Shin, Director of Publications
National Educational Service
1610 West Third Street
P.O. Box 8
Bloomington, IN 47402
1-800-733-6786
1-812-336-7700

FOR FURTHER ASSISTANCE ON
SCHOOL BASED MANAGEMENT
- Facilitator Training
- School Plans
- School Budgets
- Advisory Committee Training
- Budget Decentralization
- Management Training

CONTACT:
Neal Associates
P.O. Box 1026
Falls Church, VA 22041
(703) 820-7612

NEED MORE COPIES?

Need more copies of this book? Want your own copy? If so, you can order additional copies of *School Based Management: A Detailed Guide for Successful Implementation* by using this form or by calling us TOLL FREE at 1-800-733-6786.

We guarantee complete satisfaction with all of our materials. If you are not completely satisfied with any NES publication, you may return it to us within 60 days for a full refund.

	Quantity	Total Price
School Based Management: A Detailed Guide for Successful Implementation ($21.95 each)	_____	_____
Shipping: Add $1.50 per copy (There is no shipping charge when you *include* payment with your order)		_____
Indiana residents add 5% sales tax		_____
TOTAL		_____

❏ Check enclosed with order   ❏ Please bill me
❏ Money Order   ❏ VISA or MasterCard

Account No._____ Exp. Date _____
Cardholder _____
Ship to:
Name_____Title _____
Organization _____
P.O.# _____
Address _____
City _____
State_____ ZIP _____
Phone Number_____

MAIL TO:
National Educational Service
1610 W. Third Street
P.O. Box 8
Bloomington, IN 47402

School Based Management: A Detailed Guide for Successful Implementation is one of the many publications produced by the National Educational Service. Our mission is to provide you and other leaders in education, business, and government with timely, top-quality publications, videos, and conferences. If you have any questions or comments about *School Based Management* or any of our other publications or services, please contact us at:

National Educational Service
1610 W. Third Street
P.O. Box 8
Bloomington, IN 47402
(812) 336-7700
(800) 733-6786

LB
2805
.N464
1991